T·H·E·S·E F·O·R
R·E·M·E·M·B·R·A·N·C·E

MEMOIRS OF 6 FRIENDS KILLED IN THE GREAT WAR

JOHN BUCHAN

Introduction by
PETER VANSITTART

BUCHAN & ENRIGHT, PUBLISHERS
LONDON

Privately printed 1919

First published in a general edition by
Buchan & Enright, Publishers, Limited
53 Fleet Street, London EC4Y 1BE

British Library Cataloguing in Publication Data

Buchan, John, *1875–1940*
These for remembrance: memoirs of six
friends killed in the Great War.
1. World War, 1914–1918—Biography
2. Great Britain—Biography
I. Title
920.71'0941   DA566.9.A1

ISBN 0-907675-80-8

Printed in Great Britain by
Richard Clay Ltd, Bungay, Suffolk

THESE FOR REMEMBRANCE

PUBLISHER'S NOTE

John Buchan wrote *These For Remembrance* immediately after the Great War had ended in 1918 (the title would seem to be an echo of Ophelia's 'That's for remembrance' in *Hamlet*). The book was privately printed in 1919 by monotype letterpress on hand-made paper, the illustrations being original photographs glued by hand on to the relevant pages, or drawings by Blackwood glued or bound in. The work was supervised by the Medici Society, and carried out at the Chiswick Press. Quite how many copies were produced is not known, but it is unlikely to have been more than seven; one for John Buchan himself, and one each for the families of the six men whose lives he had commemorated. It is possible, however, that Buchan's was the only complete copy, and that each of his friends' families was given only the relevant section from the complete book. Hand-printing and -binding then, as now, were prohibitively expensive.

The text and illustrations of *These For Remembrance* printed here are exact reproductions of the originals, and have been printed by offset-lithography from John Buchan's own copy, maintaining the original type sizes. The author's personal copy was hand-bound by Katherine Adams, FRSA (Mrs Edmund Webb, born 1862), the foremost book-binder of her day, whose work included Queen Mary's prayer book for the coronation of her husband, King George V, in 1911. The original book measures $12\frac{1}{2}$ inches in depth by $8\frac{1}{4}$ inches across, and is full bound in reddish-brown morocco, blocked in gold on the front and back boards, as well as the spine, and with all three paper edges trimmed and gilded. The front board is blocked with the title, the shield from the Buchan coat-of-arms, and a decorative border.

CONTENTS

INTRODUCTION

Peter Vansittart

'The kernel of romance is contrast, beauty and valour flowering in unlikely places, the heavenly rubbing shoulders with the earthly. The true romantic is not the Byronic hero; he is the British soldier whose idea of a *beau geste* is to dribble a football into the enemy's trenches.'

JOHN BUCHAN

John Buchan was part of a versatile tradition in which a novelist could become Prime Minister, and his successors publish books on philosophy, translations of Homer, biographies of Pitt, Napoleon, Marlborough: when a Lord Chancellor produced such works as *The Pathway to Reality*, *The Reign of Relativity*, *The Philosophy of Humanism*, a First Lord be a considerable historian, journalist, wit, an India Secretary write on Diderot, on *Compromise*. A novelist could have a variety of personal experience. Maurice Baring was diplomat, translator, war correspondent, wartime air force staff officer; Saki, a political satirist, foreign correspondent, historian of the Russian Empire, wartime sergeant of infantry; A. E. W. Mason, an actor, wartime naval intelligence officer, and like Belloc, a Liberal MP; Conan Doyle, doctor, spiritualist, tireless defender of human rights and social causes, inventor, and performer of the hazardous feat of clean bowling Dr W. G. Grace; Rider Haggard, colonial administrator, farmer, pioneer of afforestation, political pamphleteer, land reformer, Parliamentary candidate, was also President of the Vegetable, Fur and Feather Society, Vice-President of the Council for Public Morals, co-signatory with Kipling for the Anti-Bolshevik

Liberty League, founded by Wickham Steed, editor of *The Times*. At twenty-one, John Masefield had been a seaman, though a bad one, and, in America, a vagrant, gardener, bartender, dogsbody in a dubious hotel, farmhand, dynamiter, and drudge in a bakery, a livery stable, and a carpet factory. Wartime secret agents included Somerset Maugham and Compton Mackenzie.

Print was not rivalled by cinema, television, radio, and authors were not reticent. Between them, Chesterton, Shaw, Belloc, Wells, Masefield, issued over five hundred books. The output of Hardy, James, Conrad, Yeats, Bennett, Woolf, Kipling, D. H. Lawrence, Ford Madox Ford, Walpole, Priestley, was not niggardly. Compton Mackenzie wrote 100 books; one of 100,000 words, in a month. Buchan himself published some eighty books. He wrote on South Africa, the Glencoe Massacre, the law of taxation of foreign income, the Royal Scots Fusiliers, Brasenose College, the Scottish Kirk, the Border Country, Canada, Lord Minto, the Great War, General Gordon, the eighteenth century, George V and much else. He wrote biographies of Raleigh, Montrose, Oliver Cromwell, Julius Caesar, Augustus, and—perhaps his best— his revered Walter Scott: he wrote short stories, novels, essays and criticism, memoirs and some verse.

He was not, like many of his intimates, born into grandeur, but was a son of a Scottish manse, scarcely impoverished but not rich: 'like most Scottish families, we believed ourselves gently born' (*Memory-Hold-The-Door*); in early days at Oxford he could not afford to dine in hall. His schooling was not Eton, not Winchester, but Hutcheson's, a Glasgow grammar school, though it was indeed one of Scotland's best and most famous schools.

This background, reinforced by Calvinist tradition and native respect for meritocracy, encouraged, indeed neces- sitated continuous work. In his teens he was reading the Sagas in Icelandic. At sixteen, he enrolled at Glasgow University.

The professor who took most interest in Buchan, and

helped most to shape his life, was Gilbert Murray, who had been appointed to the chair of Greek . . . He found Buchan 'a treasure of a pupil', gave him extra tutorials, fired him with his own enthusiasm for Sophocles, Euripides, Ibsen and social reform, and encouraged him to try for an Oxford scholarship [Janet Adam Smith, *John Buchan and his World*, 1979].

Murray was to become the father-in-law of Philip Toynbee, lifelong Buchan admirer, who founded, 1952, 'the Wednesday Club', in lively emulation of the fictional 'Thursday Club', attended by such Buchan regulars as Richard Hannay, Edward Leithen, Sandy Arbuthnot. Buchan won the scholarship, and Oxford remained a permanent part of him: its learning and quirkiness, clubs, libraries, common rooms, its eccentrics and practical jokers, its sport and countryside. Three of the six friends evoked in this book he met at Oxford. 'Every generation, I know, has the same prejudice; but I am convinced that few men have ever had more lovable, more brilliant, more generous, more gallant friends.' This view, of course, was common among many Great War survivors, though the purpose of Buchan's little book was to substantiate it.

At nineteen, he had published his first book, an edition of Bacon, and, on leaving Oxford, had produced five more. President of the Union, First in Greats, winner of the Newdigate Poetry Prize, his only serious rebuff was failure to win a Fellowship to All Souls. When still an undergraduate he was principal reader for The Bodley Head, had his berth in *Who's Who*. He was early writing not only for *Blackwood's*, the *Spectator*, the *Westminster Gazette*, but for the *Yellow Book*, years later provoking a sour comment from the ruined Wilde in a Betjeman poem: it should be remembered that Betjeman's history is at fault. Wilde was arrested in 1895. Buchan's solitary *Yellow Book* story ('At the Article of Death') appeared in Volume 12, January 1897, when he was twenty-two. This was the year of Wilde's release.

'So you've brought me the latest *Yellow Book*:
And Buchan has got in it now:

Approval of what is approved of
Is as false as a well-kept vow.'

Buchan's detractors might have relished the remark of his
fellow Scot, James Barrie, to the effect that there is no sight
more deeply impressive than that of a Scotsman on the make.
His detractors have also made much of the lists of 'Things to
be done in the next 4 years' and of 'Honours gained and to be
gained', which he compiled while at Oxford. What is perhaps
most extraordinary about these is just how many of his ambitions
he achieved. Subsequently, Buchan was variously journalist,
barrister, Curator of the Oxford University Chest, personal
assistant to Lord Milner in South Africa helping in reconstruc-
tion after the Boer War, Lord High Commissioner of the General
Assembly of the Church of Scotland, Tory MP, Privy Council-
lor, Chancellor of Edinburgh University, Trustee of the Pilgrim
Trust, publisher, assistant editor of the *Spectator*, deputy chair-
man of Reuters, 'Atticus' on the *Sunday Times*, editor of the
Scottish Review, lieutenant-colonel in the Intelligence Corps, a
director of Military Intelligence and of the wartime Ministry of
Information, itself largely modelled on his suggestions, where
he employed such writers as Arnold Bennett, Hugh Walpole,
Henry Newbolt, Anthony Hope, and influenced the appointment of Orpen, Paul Nash, Sargent, Nevinson, Steer as war
artists. His friends, none of whom he allowed too close, included
Chaim Weizmann, T. E. Lawrence and Stanley Baldwin. He
was mountaineer, in 1914 planning with Cecil Rawling to
attempt Everest; bird watcher, fisherman, walker, and, as Chief
of the Big Mountain, and Chief Man from Above who Has
Come to Help Us, honorary member of two tribes of Canadian
Indians. He died when Governor-General of Canada, 1940.

All this, somewhat daunting to more casual spirits, scarcely
suggests immediate sympathy with Wilde's dictum, that to do
nothing is the most difficult thing in the world and quite the
most intelligent. G. M. Trevelyan, himself no limpet, wrote
(1947) that in Buchan's presence he always felt ashamed that
he was not more active.

Buchan has been derided as seeking success, hunting pots, yet in his work he was attracted to nonconformists, independents, the losers and half-losers: Raleigh, Charles I, Montrose, even Cromwell, and to the constraints and limitations of power and success. In *John Macnab*, three forbiddingly grand public men risk name and reputation by a calculated prank, ostensibly urchin-like, but in essence a snook cocked at convention, akin to the defiant contempt which made T. E. Lawrence, infuriated by the Versailles Peace Settlement, bombard Paris from the air with cushions. (This was akin, too, to Orpen's now-destroyed painting of the Versailles Conference, when, furious at its deliberations and remoteness, he painted out all the leaders and put, in the setting of the Salle des Glâces, a coffin on trestles, draped with a Union Jack, and beside it, two dead, almost naked, blown-up British Tommies, trailing bandages and rags of clothing.) One wonders how much Buchan regarded himself as a success. He had, of course, to make his way amongst groups whose ways, incomes, nationalities, were at odds with his own.

Similarly, he sympathised with minorities: Eskimoes, Red Indians, and was a steadfast Zionist. Zionism was 'a great act of justice, reparation for centuries of cruelty and wrong which have stained the record of nearly every Gentile people'. He has been abused for anti-Jewish remarks, mild enough and typical of their pre-Hitler day, made by his fictional characters. Less familiar are Janet Adam Smith's words: 'His name was written in the Golden Book of the Jewish National Fund of Israel, to be honoured along with such other friends of Israel as Smuts, Balfour, Amery and Orde Wingate.' He was a friend of the 'Clydeside Reds,' Maxton, McGovern, Kirkwood: confidant not only of Baldwin but of Ramsay MacDonald, and, when Governor-General, befriended Canadian left-wingers. Friendship, like religion, nature, sex, literature, revoked party lines.

Buchan was a classicist, familiar with Greek and Latin languages and history, not as escape into a dead past but as another access to the live present. From boyhood excursions in Walter Scott's Border regions, from his work and journeying throughout South Africa, from his reading, and from his religion and family background, he understood the relevance of history. History was a tool in the conflict of nations and classes, ideas and prejudices: was source of warnings, analogies, omens and stories, the tragic, the comic. For him the past was continuous and inescapable; he would have agreed with Croce that all history is contemporary history. A man without memory would have a life exciting but probably dangerous. History, social memory, in Buchan's work, is always hovering, clear-cut or poetically allusive, the reader always in the middle. It is as hard as physics and technology, sad as the scaffold, solid as the Tower, and with glimpses of imps and jesters. A stone circle on a windy moor can speak louder than dictators. G. K. Chesterton, his contemporary, remarked that it takes an age which has nothing to say to invent the loudspeaker. What Buchan reported of Walter Scott could apply also to his own rigorous common sense. 'If he was told that such and such a thing was in accordance with the spirit of the age, he replied that the spirit of the age might be a lying spirit, with no claim to infallibility.'

Buchan, born 1875, with a duodenal ulcer since 1912, knew persistent pain and, despite an exceptionally happy marriage and loving family, had his share of grief, the gist of this book. Religious, he could also be considered a Stoic: it can be overlooked that the Stoics emphasised not only personal virtue and universality, transcendence of faction, sect, school, but expression of virtue through action. Like them, he had a controlled personality, a controlled talent. Maxim Gorky described a Russian soldier bursting into laughter when companions beside him were abruptly blown to pieces, their remains scattered over a tree. 'Naturally, a little later, I began feeling rather bad about it. After all, they were my comrades, chaps just like me. And now, suddenly—not a scrap of them anymore—as if they'd not lived at all. But at first—I laughed.' Buchan is unimaginable doing likewise. Nor can he be likened to Knut Hamsun, great novelist, pro-Hitler traitor, who, finishing a book, would remain drunk for weeks, 'as a means of destroying the unusable remains of a finished book in his head and clearing space for the next' (Robert Ferguson, 1987). Catherine Carswell (in *John Buchan By His Wife and Friends*, 1947) suspected, rightly, that about Buchan's mouth lurked not laughter but a hint of subdued pain. His internal torment, overwork, stupendous attention to the needs of others, the loss of loved ones, all must have contributed, and, though he possessed humour, at such things he could not laugh.

As Governor-General, his peak of outward success, he was extraordinarily positive, no passive rubber stamp but covering huge areas of the Dominion in an effort to promote national awareness and unity, within the menace of world war, as well as to assuage his unflagging curiosity. 'Without curiosity,' wrote Ezra Pound, a very different type, 'there can be no literature.' It could be said that the ending of the Great War had turned Buchan away from Europe towards North America, and the Canadian appointment allowed him perhaps the fullest possible outlet for the new range of interests. In return, Buchan had some hand in the 1938 Roosevelt peace proposals, pointedly ignored in Europe, not least by Britain.

Like that of most authors, much of Buchan's writing concerns the conflict of opposites, or seeming opposites. Town against country, royalist against cavalier, virtue against treachery, order against conspiracy. It suggests naivety, though its workings can be complex enough for one who aimed to attract and please a big audience. This indeed he did, appealing to the oldest of literary themes. 'Action was his prime interest, and men in action his absorbing study—most of all, men in heroic action' (Carswell). He seemed fascinated by what Arnold Toynbee termed Withdrawal and Return: the historical phenomenon of a hero, leader, messiah, through defeat, weariness, despondency, forsaking men and cities for the wilderness, not for always, but to recharge himself, prepare for a triumphant restoration. In Buchan's novels, danger and anonymity in some fateful mission can be an antidote to fame, glamour, inertia. Also, a figure, enigmatic, perhaps sinister, may remove disguise and reveal himself as Sandy Arbuthnot: at next remove, his stories, his biographies, may concern men self-divided, at moral or political crossroads. Gertrude Himmelfarb ('John Buchan', *Encounter*, 1960) asserts, 'In history, as in fiction, his heroes were by no means the simple clean-cut men of action who shoulder their way to victory. They were sensitive souls, fated to noble failures and pyrrhic victories.' She shows them as often introspective, inclined to self-doubt despite their wordly distinction.

They may also, like their creator, emerge from quarters very much at odds with founder members of the Thursday Club. Peter Pienaar, Mr Blenkiron, Dickson McCunn, Hannay himself were not born into the celebrated Buchan world of coteries, élites, clubs: the successful. Himmelfarb justly cites Hannay in *Mr Standfast*, a general, wholeheartedly supporting the Great War, yet saluting the dead conscientious objector, Launcelot Wake. 'If the best were to be taken, he would be chosen first, for he was a big man, before whom I uncovered my head.' Here Hannay, and surely Buchan himself, seems acknowledging a vital, if private part of a self more than usually public.

'Human beings,' Buchan reflected (*Memory Hold-the-Door*, 1940) 'were compounded with both heavenly and hellish elements with infinite possibilities of sorrow and joy. In consequence I had an acute sense of sin and a strong hatred of whatever debased human nature.' The influence of his upbringing, and particularly of his mother, seems relevant here.

This pervades his histories and fiction. As a historian, he was praised by authorities as diverse as G. M. Trevelyan and A. L. Rowse. Himmelfarb considered:

The portraits of Montrose and Cromwell in Buchan's excellent biographies, are also tributes to the complicated man who is torn by conflicting ideas and emotions and barely manages to maintain a precarious balance: Montrose, starting as a Covenanter in rebellion against the king, and ending as the 'noblest cavalier', while still a Presbyterian;

Cromwell, the 'practical mystic', the revolutionist with a passion for law and order, the leader who is a prey to withdrawal and self-doubt.

Narrative and character, personal adaptation to crisis and change, conflict of loyalties, are Buchan' insights, rather than class analysis, social detail and statistics, universal generalisations. Despite personal antipathies and sympathies, he treated his protagonists fairly, in the classical tradition of giving each god his due, an overall appreciation of human personality. He would produce an acute phrase for whatever touched his own being. On Calvinism (in *Montrose*), he reflected, 'Historically its importance lay in its absoluteness, for a religion which becomes a "perhaps" will not stand in the day of battle.' In *Cromwell*, he wrote of Laud, 'He applied the brain of a college pedant to the spacious life of England.' *Spacious* is revealing.

His fiction, seldom very ambitious, was liable to attack as melodramatic and unrealistic. 'It is well written,' Lady Cynthia Asquith, (who was married to Raymond's brother) commented on *The Thirty-Nine Steps*, 'and quite fun, but too full of glaring improbabilities, not to say impossibilities.' Theme and atmosphere can outweigh plot, but accusations of impossibility were more plausible in the days of the League of Nations, the Kellogg Pact to outlaw war, the impact of Gandhi, the growth of pacificism and trust in liberal advance. Present-day readers might more easily accept Buchan's premises. Consider the following:

Among his most outstanding characteristics were a strict attention to detail, unselfishness, love of Nature, sentimentality, even a certain helpfulness and kindliness, simplicity, and finally a marked hankering after morality.

Of whom was this written? King Alfred? Dr Watson? Orwell? George V? Actually, of Commandant Höss of Auschwitz, lover of Mozart, literature and horses, and, after

Hitler, Himmler and Stalin, the greatest mass-killer since Genghis Khan. Yet the citation would not have astonished Buchan, creator of Dominick Medina, MP, poet, charmer, sportsman, popular and intelligent clubman, member of the Thursday Club élite, but also kidnapper, hypnotist, potential terrorist and murderer, obscurantist, and vengeful, mindless nationalist, dedicated to the destruction of British society. Buchan's sense of reality was as deeply grounded as that of fellow-writers more generally acclaimed: Wells, with heroic visions of man stepping from star to star, yet long under-estimating the powers of unreason; Shaw, genial, often wise, with a keen nose for capitalist scoundrels, tossing off fuses to illuminate or shock—he once, in a Labour pamphlet, advocated the gassing of incurable criminals—but who could not recognise evil when he met it face to face. 'Stalin has delivered the goods to an extent that seemed impossible ten years ago; and I take off my hat to him accordingly' (1934). The 'goods' included the corpses of some millions of his fellow citizens and a sizeable proportion of his own Party colleagues. Buchan, who served on Haig's staff, would have queried W. B. Yeats's confession that he found that the Great War 'did not have much reality', and he was surely shocked by H. H. Asquith, classicist, ex-Premier, father of his admired friend Raymond, declaring that the war had cleansed and purged the world. He himself noted the anti-climactic nature and 'sinister secrecy' of trench warfare.

The Three Hostages (1924) contains conversation at the Thursday Club in which Hannay, the narrator, with Sandy Arbuthnot and Medina, are joined by such men—the Club would outrage feminists and egalitarians—as

a wizened little man who had just returned from bird-hunting at the mouth of the Mackenzie. There was Palliser-Yeates, the banker who didn't look thirty, and Fulleylove, the Arabian traveller, who was really thirty and looked fifty. I was specially interested in Nightingale, a slim peering fellow with double glasses, who had gone back to Greek manuscripts and his Cambridge fellowship after captaining a Beduin tribe. Leithen was there too, the Attorney-General, who had been a private in the Guards at the start of the war, and had finished up as a G.S.O.I., a toughly built man with a pale face and very keen quizzical eyes. I should think there must have been more varied and solid brains in that dozen than you would find in an average Parliament.

The conversation cannot be condemned as romantic or archaic.

We would have drifted into politics, if Pugh had not asked him [Sandy] his opinion of Gandhi. This led him into an exposition of the meaning of the fanatic, a subject on which he was well-qualified to speak, for he had consorted with most varieties.

'He is always in the technical sense mad—that is, his mind is tilted from its balance, and since we live by balance he is a wrecker, a crowbar in the machinery. His power comes from the appeal he makes to the imperfectly balanced, and as these are never the majority his appeal is limited. But there is one kind of fanatic whose strength comes from balance, from a lunatic balance. You cannot say that there is any one thing abnormal about him, for he is all abnormal. He is as balanced as you or me, but, so to speak, in a fourth dimensional world. That kind of man has no logical gaps in his creed. Within his insane postulates he is brilliantly sane. Take Lenin for instance. That's the kind of fanatic I'm afraid of.'

Leithen asked how such a man got his influence. 'You say that there is no crazy spot in him which appeals to a crazy spot in other people.'

'He appeals to the normal,' said Sandy solemnly, 'to the perfectly sane. He offers reason, not visions—in any case his visions are reasonable. In ordinary times he will not be heard, because, as I say, his world is not our world. But let there come a time of great suffering or discontent, when the mind of the ordinary man is in desperation, and the rational fanatic will come by his own. When he appeals to the sane and the sane respond, revolutions begin.'

Pugh nodded his head, as if he agreed. 'Your fanatic of course must be a man of genius.'

'Of course. And genius of that kind is happily rare. When it exists, its possessor is the modern wizard. The old necromancer fiddled away with caballistic signs and crude chemicals and got nowhere; the true wizard is the man who works by spirit on spirit. We are only beginning to realise the strange crannies of the human soul. The real magician, if he turned up to-day, wouldn't bother about drugs and dopes. He would dabble in far more deadly methods, the compulsion of a fiery nature over the limp things that men call their minds.'

Some years later, Adolf Hitler was declaiming:

The masses need something that will give them a thrill of power . . . A new age of magical interpretation of the world is at hand, of interpretation in terms of the will and not of the intelligence.

Subsequent revelations from archives and the Nuremberg trials, not only of master war-criminals but of corrupt monopolies, international cartels, cowardly bureaucracies, bribed parliaments, show that Buchan's 'shockers', involving world conspiracies, subsidised terrorism, bolshevik or nihilistic fanaticism, moles in high places, if sometimes clumsily presented, were not as preposterous as they might have seemed in the immediate wake of 'the war that will end war', a notion of H. G. Wells invalidated by subsequent events.

A more serious limitation of Buchan's imagination is that it offered itself as almost exclusively masculine. Few of his women are more than insipid or stock: most of them Gertrude Bell, Freya Stark, Sylvia Pankhurst, Mary Kingsley, Eleanor Marx, Eleanora Duse, Lady Gregory, Alexandra Kollentai, would have cracked across their knees and eaten. Of fictional women, Tolstoy's Natasha seems to have been Buchan's favourite, but he never attempted a personality so live and convincing.

Nevertheless, his work under Milner in South Africa,

helping to reconcile the Boers, rebuild, achieve new land settlements, his dealings in the 'concentration camps', their fearful mortality and enduring resentments, his criss-cross travels, minor adventures, encounters with manifold human types, coloured not only his romanticism but allowed much hard grit of actuality. His was an individualism tempered by responsibility: imagination tested against practical experience. Like Alain-Fournier, he enjoyed the fantastic only within the real.

Though alert to the developments of the modern world, he was no modernist. He read Freudians with, one imagines, interest but detachment, keeping his head, retaining his ego. No determinist, he was not tempted to discredit a coherent and lasting self. Around him, art, science, philosophy, linguistics were undermining Renaissance Man, as Galileo, Bruno, Copernicus, Brahe, Kepler, Bacon, Newton—telescope, microscope, mathematics, experiment—had Gothic Man. Alongside, or deriving from, the Quantum Theory, Relativity, Comparative Religion, Anthropology, the splitting of the atom, was the atomising of total experience, fragmentation of personality, fusion of the archaic and futuristic, myth and psychology, fairy tale and dream, primitive symbols and modern belief, the abrasive, sceptical minimising of inherited ideals and absolute values. In politics, traditional authority was questioned, mocked, or overthrown, its successors were stabilised by dogmas, tribunal, capital punishment, ritual slogans, secret police, under new and high-sounding names. In literature, Beauty, so craved by Bridges, Masefield, Buchan himself, was redefined, redesigned, by Kipling, by Ezra Pound and T. S. Eliot, and older conceptions of romance and human nature were shattered by the prolonged torture of the Great War.

General Wavell selected a Buchan poem for his anthology, *Other Men's Flowers* (1944). Dedicated to his brother Willie, it begins:

> When we were little, wandering boys,
> And every hill was blue and high,

On ballad ways and martial joys
   We fed our fancies, you and I.
With Bruce we crouched in bracken shade,
   With Douglas charged the Paynim foes,
And oft in moorland noons I played
   Colkitto to your grave Montrose.

The obliterating seasons flow—
   They cannot kill our boyish game.
Though creeds may change and kings may go,
   Yet burns undimmed the ancient flame.
While young men in their pride make haste
   The wrong to right, the bond to free,
And plant a garden in the waste,
   Still rides our Scottish chivalry.

Buchan lived on into an era in which the Somme, Gallipoli, Tannenberg, Verdun, outmoded such imagery. Right, wrong, 'the waste', the nature of freedom, had to submit to scrupulous analysis, often with disconcerting results. Chivalry was exposed as an elaborate and hypocritical disguise for a brutal, over-masculine age. The Crusaders were vicious, land-hungry invaders and political intriguers. Heroines did not always fare better. Charlotte Corday, Jane Grey, were found chilly and unlovable, as obsessed as their oppressors. In many homes, toy soldiers would be replaced by *Monopoly*, though, to anti-capitalists, this was no obvious advance. (Tin pacifists, Orwell observed, somehow wouldn't do.) Buchan's ancient, undimmed flame would tempt certain disrespectful fellows to extinguish it. G.B.S. was not alone in demanding new games, new rules:

> After profound reflection I have come to the conclusion that mankind is fit for nothing better than the chasing of a ball about the field. Perhaps in another thousand years it may prove equal to the moral and intellectual task of kicking the ball out of the field.

The Finnish poet Edith Södergram, in idiom and technique, started from bases very different from Buchan's.

> I want to forget my manners—
> I couldn't care less about noble styles,
> I roll up my sleeves.
> The dough of poetry is rising . . .
> Oh, what a sorrow—I can't bake cathedrals.

Nor could Buchan, though he might never have contemplated doing so, and his sorrow would have been perfunctory. For the rest of his life he probably preferred to quote Belloc, Chesterton, Baring, rather than Eliot and Pound. His verse is unlikely to be reprinted. His fiction survives better. Novels and stories are set in many different periods onwards from Vikings and Normans, with back-glances to Greece and Rome. Many display his feeling for nature and landscape. Walter Elliot observed that 'he could write about the small hidden green valleys of the Borders until they closed around you,' (*John Buchan By His Wife and Friends*). Also about Oxfordshire, Canada, Turkey, Germany, France, Norway. His technique may be slow and discursive to readers and writers trained by the cinema to swift cross-cutting, delicate flashbacks, elaborate shiftings of space and time, often at the expense of sheer narrative, but for this last he still secures readers. It remains arguable whether the screen versions of *The Thirty-Nine Steps*—dedicated to Tommy Nelson, 1915—actually improved the story. He found significance, 'romance' not only in Viking forays, Saxon defeats, in pagan witchcraft and sectarian hatreds, in escapes through glens, and drama on hillsides. Reviewing his last novel, *Sick Heart River*, Graham Greene wrote (1941):

> John Buchan was the first to realise the enormous dramatic value of adventure in familiar surroundings happening to unadventurous men, members of Parliament and members of the Athenaeum, lawyers and barristers, business men and minor peers: murder in the atmosphere of breeding and simplicity and stability: Richard Hannay, Sir Edward Leithen, Archie Roylance, and Lord Lamancha; these were his adventurers, not Dr Nikola or the Master of Ballantrae,

and who will forget the first thrill in 1916 as the hunted Leithen—the future Solicitor-General—ran 'like a thief in a London thoroughfare on a June afternoon'?

'Now I saw how thin is the protection of our civilization. An accident and a bogus ambulance—a false charge and a bogus arrest—there were a dozen ways of spiriting one out of this gay and bustling world.'

Buchan, though no psychological initiate, yet knew that opposites could fuse, fair be foul, foul be fair and, like love, like 999-year leases, titles, reputation and the normal are provisional. Dick Hannay, after that Thursday Club dinner talk, walks with Medina through London streets, having mentioned queer places he had shared with Sandy.

The memory of those queer places came back to me as we walked across Berkeley Square. The West End of London always affected me with a sense of the immense solidity of our civilization. These great houses, lit and shuttered and secure, seemed the extreme opposite of the world of half-lights and perils in which I had sometimes journeyed. I thought of them as I thought of Fosse Manor [his home], as sanctuaries of peace. But to-night I felt differently towards them. I wondered what was going on at the back of those heavy doors. Might not terror and mystery lurk behind that barricade as well as in tent and slum? I suddenly had a picture of a plump face all screwed up with fright, muffled beneath the bed-clothes.

Far from convinced that the Great War had made the world safe for democracy, as the American President, historian, idealistic, but ignorant of Europe and of political psychology, had hoped, Buchan more than ever sensed barbarians lurking on the frontier and, as in late Roman days, with dangerous appeal to the debt-ridden, declassed, over-taxed, the bored, the dispirited, degenerate and mischievous. Publisher, traveller, politician, he kept abreast of post-war developments other than political. In such novels as *The Dancing Floor* and *The Gap in the Curtain*, he recognised the powers of myth, the unconscious and irrational, hypnosis, the dualism suppressed, but still extant within orthodox, monotheistic religion; the recurrence of prophetic dreams, the lure of defeat and wreckage, and symbols, ancient but abiding, by which people live, without always knowing it. He had always kept his eyes open and noticed too that 'brilliant, open-handed men slip into dark morasses from which they sometimes never emerge'. In such novels abound references to people, places, actions, from the inescapable Great War.

John Buchan was born into a Europe still largely Christian and monarchical, with France and Germany still smouldering from the monstrous and unnecessary 1870 war. Empires, Europe itself, were governed by a comparatively small network of men, types met in Buchan novels. He himself has been called Victorian, though the label, while handy, is incomplete. How Victorian, indeed, was Victoria? Perhaps surprisingly, Victoria and the Empress Eugénie, for example, were pro-Dreyfus, and the far more intellectual Princess Mathilde was the reverse. (Buchan's sympathies should, by now, appear obvious.) Marx preferred the 'reactionary' Balzac to the 'democratic' Zola. What should be often is not. He always, however, remained a little outside what Raymond Asquith called the passion for noise and novelty and nonsense (he himself referred to the *rastaqouère* of the Edwardian age, employing a French word for a flashy adventurer). He was disinclined to experiment very far, though he enjoyed the novels of Virginia Woolf, so very different from his own, and set 'O Mistress Mine' to jazz. A Tory, he was no die-hard, but he believed in the organic, the well-established, the traditional institutions of throne and altar, elected assemblies, law, not as infallible guarantees of the good and the gracious, nor as bulwarks of repression, but as working compromises between past and future, absolutism and the Commune, largely fitting the needs of general human nature. They were scarcely romantic. Exciting government is usually bad government. Like the friends he describes in this book, he did not desire the Perfect State, he wanted better government. Romantic himself, he was no utopian.

He believed in property, not for privilege and rents, but as creative opportunity, an islet of hospitality—he and his wife were famous for this—a pledge to the future. A system by which he himself could, from small origins, end as royal representative and peer, he would not condemn as stifling and rigid. Authority was needful, not as inherited licence to irresponsibility or sinecures, but as personal responsibility to be earned, and, if abused, forfeited. Julius Caesar and Augustus, seen as restorers of order after material breakdown, political catastrophe, moral confusion, were likely subjects for his pen: he is less readily imagined devoting himself to Catiline, Attila, Hitler. He did not over-reverence the institutions. 'The English public school system is the only one which fits a man for life and ruins him for eternity.' Pacific, but no pacifist, he admired the old Regular Army, which had 'a kind of humorous realism about life, a dislike of tall talk, a belief in inherited tradition and historic ritual, a rough and ready justness, a deep cheerfulness which was not inconsistent with a surface pessimism.' He enjoyed titles, illustrious names and households, less from vulgar snobbery and careerism than for their historical weight, their links with a Britain whose merits he may have romanticised but, as a Hannay or Arbuthnot might put it, had made some show in the world. It had after all, invented a concept unique, and still not lovingly accepted by the greater part of humanity, not that of a crusade, empire, bombs, but of legal, indeed paid, Opposition. Latter-day revolutions, identified not only with equality but with the secret police and the scaffold, he would have rated progress backwards. He mentions, often enough, the divide between civilization and barbarism, 'a line, a thread, a sheet of glass', and considered—surely rather questionable—that true barbarism, presumably Vikings and Goths, Zulus and Red Indians, was 'a noble state' since such people had never learnt better. What he loathed and feared was 'de-civilisation': civilised people losing their way and returning to barbarism.

'The Nazis,' George Orwell wrote, 'used science in the cause of superstition.'

The pre-1914 of Buchan's youth and emergence was no sunlit afternoon of endless cucumber sandwiches and languid witticisms, but of growing European unrest, an era of Slavonic and Fenian murders, mass strikes often bloodily smashed, apocalyptic threats. In January 1885, Fenians attempted to blow up the Tower of London and the House of Commons. There had been ample warnings of the catastrophe which eliminated Buchan's six friends. The 1870 war and Commune, Paris littered with 20,000 executed civilians; the swift destruction of a technological 'masterpiece', the *Titanic*, complete but for binoculars, lifeboats and common sense ('God Himself couldn't sink this ship'); the Winter Palace Massacre; and the obliteration by the Japanese of the Imperial Russian fleet at Tsu-Shima. Buchan himself, Governor-General, declared to the Canadians:

> Look back to the years before the Great War. Our first thought about them is that, in the retrospect they seem a time of unbelievable ease and prosperity. Yes, but if we probe into our memory we shall find that they were uncomfortable years. The world was arrogant and self-satisfied, but, behind all its confidence there was an uneasy sense of impending disaster. The old creeds, both religious and political, were largely in process of dissolution, but we did not realise the fact, and therefore did not look for new foundations. Well, the war, with its abysmal suffering and destruction, did achieve one thing. It revealed us to ourselves. It revealed how thin the crust was between a complex civilization and primeval anarchy.

The six portraits Buchan gives here should be read with this speech in mind.

Nevertheless, 1870–1914 saw marvellous hopes for what Luigi Bazini has called the only art worth learning but which can never really be mastered, the art of inhabiting the earth. In housing, public health, social reform ... abolition of torture . . . in science, in the arts . . . was astonishing ad·ance, experiment, zest. 'Then came the war and the old life passed away in a night. We were back in an elemental region of death and hazard and sacrifice, where fortitude was to be tested in the ancient way.'

The Great War, Lloyd George considered, made the world shell-shocked. How far it recovered can still be passionately disputed. Buchan, not only a historian of the war but one who saw more of it than most historians, 'blundering into the German machine-guns' in an attempt to reach Cecil Rawling, was too tolerant and humane, despite his personal losses, to indulge in the Hun-bashing which disfigured so much wartime civilian life. His relatively sympathetic impression of Wilhelm II, making a somewhat contrived appearance in *Greenmantle*, may have startled some patriotic eyebrows in 1916, bloodshot year of Verdun, Kut, the Somme.

One casualty of that war was a particular cast of mind, wit, even perhaps facial expression, shared by many of Buchan's lordlier contemporaries. They were nurtured in Classical Languages, history, and with something of what appeared the pre-Christian outlook: disdainful of danger of death, of the caprice of gods never wholly admirable, addiction to sport and open spaces, an eloquent cult of romantic male friendships and tendency to petrify women into housekeepers or idealise them into goddesses, a personal elegance and self-assurance which enabled them to shed tears in public without shame or awkwardness.

Some writers have linked this directly with a Housman-like hankering for death and doomed youth; with the 1914 smash-up providing cannon-fodder docile or romantic, led by dare-devil officers of unimaginative irresponsibility. This and the support of patriotic verse, chauvinistic journalism, slovenly religion, inhibited mass protest and allowed the Hannays and Roylances—the Bulldog Drummonds, Hughie Marrables, and a Biggles—to lead ignorant unfortunates into the slaughter. There may be some uncomfortable truth here, but a glance at the militaristic élites abroad, the Hegelian theorists, noisy rulers, and educational systems very different from the British, would reduce the measure of British war-guilt. Certainly, the six lives recorded here give no support for a belief in upper-class callousness, militarism, immoderate greed, embryo fascism.

None had first-class intellects likely to make a major break-through in art, science, politics, the professions, despite talents, courage, wide interests, and indeed access to the eminent. Raymond Asquith's father was Prime Minister. None were born in circumstances that made death from starvation very probable. They did have a roundness of being, giving each god his due: sport and learning, emotions and intellect, danger and security. The ghost of the Scholar-Gypsy lingered amongst them. They may have been less casual than they cared to appear, but they disliked solemnity and had a taste for practical jokes. Their friend Aubrey Herbert, Bron Lucas's cousin, once dropped from a plum tree on to a tea party, 'because I was ripe'. Of him, Buchan wrote (1923), 'The most delightful and brilliant survivor from the days of chivalry . . . the most extraordinary combination of tenderness and gentleness, with insane gallantry that I have ever known—a sort of survivor from crusading armies. I drew Sandy in *Greenmantle* from him.'

Much of Buchan is in that: the romantic, the friend, the novelist, the adventurer. In 1914, Herbert, though almost blind, a military reject, ordered himself a uniform and joined the Irish Guards by stepping unnoticed into their ranks as they marched to their troop train. Had he done so in a Buchan novel, this would have been condemned as clumsily improbable. He and C.B. Fry are the only Englishmen known to have refused the throne of Albania.

'Stuffy' was a pejorative common to the Herberts, Asquiths, Nelsons and the rest. Robespierre's sermon, 'the People are sublime' they would not have accepted to the letter though, in war, they cared whole-heartedly for their men, and were returned respect, and more. Their jargon, their wit, would seem coolly insolent, over-contemptuous, to present-day feminists and egalitarians, haters of racism and imperialism, and to those for whom a classical scholarship, individualism, verbal facility, are forms of delinquency.

Nor, of course, were they impeccable. Gilded youth has temptation towards selfishness, the facile and superficial, the taking for granted of applause, personal service, an over-reliance on charm. Dislike of rules, pomposity, busybodies, could induce too spontaneous a disregard of those who, in politics and administration, oil the wheels and locks. Amongst Fabians and Suffragettes, Buchan's words might have roused irritation. 'Each of us would have rejoiced to ride over the world's edge but it would have been not for a cause but for the fun of the riding.'

Their laureate was another Oxford friend, Hilaire Belloc.

> From quiet homes and first beginning,
> Out to the undiscovered ends,
> There's nothing worth the wear of winning
> But laughter and the love of friends.

The Great War has been seen as a crisis of boredom and futility, the death-wish of ruling classes, but this would have surprised these men, with minds as crowded as their days. Youth was good to them. They must have had the periodic doubts and set-backs common to all, but death appeared very far away. What does emerge from Buchan's postscripts is a certain sophisticated world-weariness, real or assumed, compounded of some scepticism or disgust with public life, and, of course, distributed in varying degrees, for while they shared much, their personalities and interests were not uni-form. Changes were at hand, to be viewed with mixed feelings. Lloyd George and Winston Churchill were making radical noises amongst the Liberals, disrespectful to Asquith's pa-trician calm. Conceivably, the Asquiths, Greys, the unruffled Balfours, had a diminished future. Labour had entered Parlia-ment. 'We cannot afford nowadays,' Raymond Asquith wrote, 'to limit our choice of Ministers to a few stuffy families with ugly faces, bad manners and a belief in the Nicene Creed. The day of the clever cad is at hand.' He added, in a tone rather typical of his breed, 'If only Englishmen had known their Aeschylus a little better, they wouldn't have hustled about the world appropriating things.'

Yet the clever cads might not be more congenial, and certainly spent little time with Aeschylus. Lloyd George, the great tribune, defended the 1916 Conscription Bill in language at which Buchan and the others would have winced: 'Compulsion is simply organised voluntary effort.' John Burns declared that LG's conscience was pure and unspotted because he never used it. When Lloyd George, 'the Man who won the War', was accused, correctly, in 1918, of lying to the Commons, Aubrey Herbert risked his political career by supporting the accusation, replying to indignant opponents, and his own constituents and followers, 'On certain occasions I choose to behave as a gentleman.' It can be added that General Maurice, who, from conscience, made the accusation about the Government wrongly blaming the British commanders for the disasters of March, 1918, and falsifying casualty figures, had his career abruptly ended for 'a breach of discipline'.

In 1916, Lloyd George and his group, Liberal and Tory, ejected Asquith, demanding more dynamic prosecution of the war, and indeed achieving it, though none of Buchan's six friends survived.

War can solve too many private problems. At school and university, Buchan's circle had won the prizes, possibly too many. There was a danger of adult life becoming an anticlimax. In 1914 they were young, but not so very young. These six, not all with full enthusiasm, had already embarked on careers: some had written a little, made love a little, explored, had adventure and mishap in foreign lands, fought in South Africa, cherished their estates. Most had political leanings but a dislike of the clichés and discipline of Party.

Parliament they accepted in its traditional role as a restraint on public opinion. None was obsessed with ambition, each needed self-fulfilment. Here again, much as he admired and loved them, Buchan was slightly apart, adopted into their set but not born into it: from the start he had had to be a professional, with definite goals, and was too busy to be undecided, sauntering, or tired of life. In her biography of Aubrey Herbert, Margaret FitzHerbert has a passage pertinent to the others, in the situation of 1914.

Aubrey's elation at England's ultimatum to Germany over Belgian neutrality was not based on an ignorant or foolhardy misunderstanding of the magnitude of the event, but on many complicated feelings which he shared with his generation. It was not that they consciously wished to die; it was not even that they were moved by strong anti-German or pro-French sentiments; nor was it bloodlust. It was more the result of their high sense of purpose and honour. They were the flower of the Empire at its zenith. They were men of talent, some of brilliance, and yet by 1914 Aubrey's contemporaries were in their thirties and none had achieved great distinction. They had nursed their promise, not fulfilled it. They were a little tired of life, and impatient with the old men. Something less than a sense of futility, but more than a spirit of restlessness was abroad. It was as if their whole lives had been a preparation for this moment and they seized it with eagerness.

As Sandy remarks in *The Island of Sheep*, 'The time, I think, has come for me to take a hand.' Something of this Buchan sensed, in his account of Tommy Nelson, and it is echoed by a young volunteer from a very different social class from the Herberts—J. B. Priestley. Priestley, by no means tired of life, would have been caustic about 'the flower of the Empire', then grumbled about the Empire itself, but his self-diagnosis was probably expressive of many.

Years later, I often asked myself why I had joined the Army. The usual explanations were no good. I was not hot with patriotic feeling. I did not believe that Britain was in any real danger. I was sorry for 'gallant little Belgium' but did not feel that she was waiting for me to rescue her. The legend of Kitchener, who pointed at us from every hoarding, had never captured me. I was not under any pressure from public opinion ... I was not carried to the recruiting office in a herd of chums, nobody thinking, everybody half-plastered; I went alone ... This was no escape to freedom and independence; I may not have known much about military life, but I was not so green. And I certainly did not see myself as a hero, whose true stature would be revealed in war; that had never been one of my illusions. What is left then to supply a motive?

Nothing, I believe now, that was rational or conscious ... I went at a signal from the unknown ... There came out of the unclouded blue of that summer, a challenge that was almost like a conscription of the spirit, little to do with King and Country and flag-waving and hip-hip-hurrah, a challenge to what we felt was our untested manhood. Other men, who had not lived as easily as we had, had drilled and marched and borne arms—couldn't we?' [*Margin Released*, 1964.]

Also to be remembered as a volunteer was Isaac Rosenberg, painter and poet, the least likely of all soldiers, short, slight, myopic, chronically absent-minded, unsoldierly to the point of farce, who volunteered, as he wrote to Eddie Marsh, not from patriotic reasons. 'Nothing can justify war ... I thought if I joined there would be the separation allowance for my mother.' He was killed on All Fools' Day 1918, a comment, sardonic or ironic, on the death of a poet.

John Buchan did not look back on the Great War as a romantic crusade. His brother Alastair had been killed at Arras in 1917; 'Much loved by his comrades', wrote his C.O., Winston Churchill. His closest friends had perished. He knew that behind optimistic headlines were men with blood bubbles instead of eyes, or reduced to a hand thrust from the mud, or a muddled shape crucified on barbed wire. Amongst much else, Buchan would have remembered Canadian soldiers ordered to dig their own graves, before assaulting Vimy

Ridge, 1917. There was no romance in the mine crater which John Masefield saw at Beaumont Hamel,

crusted and scrubbed with yellowish tetter, like sulphur or the rancid fat on meat. The inside has rather the look of meat, for it is reddish and all streaked and scabbed with this pox and with discoloured chalk. A lot of it trickles and oozes like sores discharging pus, and this liquid gathers in holes near the bottom, and is greenish and foul and has the dazed look of eyes straining upwards. [*The Old Front Line*, 1917.]

From the Front, Raymond Asquith had described

'black stumps of really the most obscene heights and thickness, craters swimming in blood and dirt, rotting and smelling bodies and rats like shadows, fattened for the Market . . .'

Courage abounded, but nobility and gallantry are not in Edmund Blunden's lines (*Poems 1914–1920*):

. . . white, we stood,
Cold certainty held our breath;
While men in the tunnels below Larch Wood
Were kicking men to death.'

Gertrude Himmelfarb, for whom Buchan 'was one of the last articulate representatives of the old England', maintains that he had no regrets for the regime destroyed by the Great War. No doubt, but much of his personal being had been torn away by his friends' deaths; and, notwithstanding war exhaustion, reconciling speeches, the League, a desire to injure was still harboured in many people outwardly smiling; a venom existing either as terrifying squatter or welcome guest. This book reflects the shock inflicted on Buchan by the war. He may have thought of the squire in Chesterton's *The Secret People*:

Our patch of glory ended, we never heard guns again,
But the squire seemed struck in the saddle, he was foolish
    as if in pain . . .
He was stricken: it may be, after all, he was stricken at
    Waterloo.

Buchan was not foolish, but he was stricken. He writes here to his children, 'I hope it will never befall you which has befallen me—to look around and find a flat emptiness.' The gaps in an address book must have been as poignant as certain lines in the *Iliad*.

He did not relapse into glumness. He knew that the art of life, though not perhaps the purpose of life, is the transformation of loss into assets: to bear witness, to persist and struggle in the old Calvinist way. Much of his zest for life remained. At sixty he was climbing a side of the Bear Mountain, hitherto unconquered, in the Canadian Arctic; writing of Augustus, that model of successful authority, though also writing his final novel, *Sick Heart River*, the last of Edward Leithen, the eminent public man grappling with physical and spiritual loneliness, with mortality, yet preserving responsibility for another. Buchan's secretary, Mrs Killick, had observed, 'His Excellency is writing a very odd book . . . so unlike him, so introspective.' Of this last period, his son, Alastair, wrote, tellingly, 'Only twice in Canada did I see the light go out of his eyes: once when endorsing a death warrant, and when signing Canada's declaration of war.' Rather surprisingly, despite the failure of reconciliation, peace, the League, despite the merging of Left and Right tyrannies in the Stalin–Hitler Pact and the renewal of world war, Buchan had not become cynical, and as Governor-General, could write what may sound strange or sententious today: 'Public life is regarded as the crown of a career, and to young men it is the worthiest ambition. Politics is still the greatest and the most honourable adventure' (1940).

That last word had remained important. He disliked the armchair manipulator who shirks personal risk.

The extent of grief for his friends cannot be fully known to the outsider, for he retained inviolate personal reticence, hiding profoundest emotions behind work and activity, leaving much to be inferred from his books. However, in the following pages he emerges more decidedly than in his autobiography, *Memory Hold-the-Door*, which says far more of others than of himself. In this he wrote:

> The war had shown that our mastery over physical forces might end in a nightmare, that mankind was becoming like an overgrown child armed with deadly weapons, a child with immense limbs and a tiny head.

For that child, he must sometimes have thought, his friends had died.

This book, written so long ago, is not subtle or oblique. It is forthright, concerned with human singularity, aborted promise, generosity of feeling. He might have agreed that empire, republic, soviet alike crash through lack of generosity.

PETER VANSITTART
September 1987

THESE FOR REMEMBRANCE

PRIVATELY PRINTED

1919

Κοινὸν γὰρ ἔρχεται
Κῦμ' ᾿Αΐδα, πέσε δ' ἀδόκητον
ἐν καὶ δοκέοντα· τιμὰ δὲ γίνεται
ὧν θεὸς ἁβρὸν αὔξει λόγον τεθνακότων.
Pindar, Nem., vii, 43.

Ah, that Sir Humfry Gilbert should be dead:
Ah, that Sir Philip Sidney should be dead:
Ah, that Sir William Sackeuill should be dead:
Ah, that Sir Richard Grenuile should be dead:
Ah, that braue Walter Deuoreux should be dead:
Ah, that the Flowre of Knighthood should be dead,
Which, maugre deadlyest Deathes, and stonyest Stones,
That coouer worthiest worth, shall neuer dy.
Gabriel Harvey, 1592.

FOR ALICE, JOHN, WILLIAM, AND
ALASTAIR BUCHAN

THIS book is written for you to read – but not yet. It is for you as you grow older, for I want you to know something about my friends who fell in the Great War.

You have all been brought up under its shadow. Alice was only six when it began, and John is not likely to remember anything before it. Billy and Alastair were born during its course – the one just before the great battle of Verdun and the other when our armies were within two months of victory. Alice, I know, remembers Tommy Nelson, and both she and John were friends of Cecil Rawling, who was Billy's godfather, and of Jack Wortley, their mother's cousin. Alastair bears the name of the closest link of all, that gallant boy who to you was more playmate than uncle, and to me seemed almost more son than brother. His grave at Arras will be for us the most precious part of what is now the Holy Land of our people. It comforts me to think that my little brother and my dearest friend gave their lives at the same hour in the same battle and are not far apart in their resting-places.

In these short chapters I have tried to set down how those friends of mine appeared to me. Every generation, I know, has the same prejudice; but I am convinced that few men have ever had more

FOR ALICE, JOHN, WILLIAM

lovable, more brilliant, more generous, more gallant friends. As Mr. Belloc, who was one of us, has written:

> . . . no one in our long decline,
> So dusty, spiteful, and divided,
> Had quite such pleasant friends as mine,
> Or loved them half as much as I did.

I do not believe that the relation between human beings called friendship can be rated too high. You will grow up to have friends of whom you will think the world, and you may prize them the more if you know what manner of men were some of those with whose friendship I was blessed. You will agree, as youth will always agree, with Mr. Belloc:

> From quiet homes and first beginning,
> Out to the undiscovered ends,
> There's nothing worth the wear of winning
> But laughter and the love of friends.

It is, perhaps, not the whole truth, but at one stage of life it should seem to be the whole truth.

There will be one difference (I hope) between your circle and mine. Mine has had to take the shock of the greatest cataclysm that the world is likely to see for many generations. I do not want you to be always thinking about the war, for the eyes of youth should be turned forward. But neither do I want you to forget it, since it is a thing for everlasting remembrance and eternal pride. The men who were at school and college just before me, my own contemporaries, and my juniors by as much as twenty years—upon them came the ends of the earth. They propped up the falling heavens and saved the world for you. But most of them died of it. I hope that will never befall you which has befallen me - to look around and find a great emptiness. The pageant of life fills the stage as before, and we have still our interest in it; but only one or two are left of the comradeship that used to fill the stalls, and nowadays there can be no pleasant supper-parties afterwards.

So I want you to cherish the memory of the war because of the price that was paid for victory - victory for you. When you realize what riches of heart and mind, what abounding zest for life, what faithfulness and courage, were bartered for six feet of French or Flemish soil, you will come to think of those years as a consecrated stage in the procession of time. And when you read the great tales of other ages, you will not thrill to them the less for remembering that a still greater and more momentous drama was played while you were beginning life, and played by your father's friends.

I have said nothing of Francis and Rivy Grenfell, Uncle Arthur's brothers, because I have written of them in another book.

TOMMY NELSON

THOMAS ARTHUR NELSON was born in Edinburgh in 1876, the elder son of the late Thomas Nelson, the publisher. He was educated at the Edinburgh Academy and University College, Oxford. At Oxford he was Captain of the University Rugby XV, playing for Oxford from 1898 to 1900, and also playing inside three-quarter for Scotland. After leaving the University he devoted himself to the business of his publishing house. At the outbreak of war he trained with his Yeomanry Regiment, the Lothians and Border Horse, and went to the front in France in September 1915. In March 1917 he joined the Tank Corps as an Intelligence Officer, and was killed by a shell at Arras on the morning of 9 April. He was thrice mentioned in despatches, and was recommended for the D.S.O. and the M.C.

TOMMY NELSON

IT is not difficult to make a picture of one whose nature is all hard lights and shadows and sharp angles. A character with anything of the fantastic or perverse in it lends itself to easy reproduction. But it is hard to draw on a little canvas the man whose nature is large and central and human, without cranks or oddities. A sentence or two will give the reader some notion of a Coleridge or a Hazlitt, but it takes the many volumes of Lockhart to set out a Walter Scott. The very simplicity and wholesomeness of such souls defy an easy summary, for they are as spacious in their effect and as generous in their essence as daylight or summer.

By what do we remember our friends? Often by a gesture, a trick of expression, some quaint phrase, or a favourite pose, or some nicety of manner. These were but trivial things in our friendship, perhaps, but they spring first to the mind in the act of recollection. But with Tommy Nelson I do not find myself thinking of such idiosyncrasies. I can recall many mannerisms of his, but it is only by an effort of thought, for they do not run to meet the memory. His presence warmed and lit up so big a region of life that in thinking of him one is

3

overwhelmed by the multitude of things which he made better by simply existing among them. If you remove a fire from a hearth, you will remember the look not so much of the blaze itself as of the whole room in its pleasant glow. The first feeling of most of us is simply that the world since April 1917 is a dingier and bleaker place than it used to be.

We first knew each other at Oxford. I wish I could draw you a picture of the Oxford of our time -the Oxfords, rather, for there were many, and, being of a nomadic habit, I ranged throughout most of them. Tommy's Oxford, the biggest and sanest of the lot, the Oxford of sport and the ordinary man, was at its best, I think, between 1896 and 1900. At least I am sure it can never have been better. For one thing it was run largely by the football and rowing sets-true sportsmen, who lived days as laborious as most scholars, and did not merely walk about in breeches and hunting-stocks and chatter about race-meetings. I have a great weakness for the "horsey" undergraduate, but there is apt to be in Oxford a bad strain of the feeble rich, who are no good to hounds, and whose interest in the greatest of sports is confined to dealings with tailors and bookmakers. Again, many of the chief sportsmen were Scots, and had the national characteristic of many-sided interests. Sport and scholarship stood in no antagonism; each respected the other, though from a distance. Tommy's world was filled with the eternal type of the plain Briton-loyal in friendship and ranking

4

bonhomie next after courage among the virtues: high-spirited: unperturbed by problems of faith or politics: absorbed in the ritual of those games which for the moment were the business of their lives: appreciative of any kind of talent but more appreciative of character: healthy in body, and with an insatiable zest for all robust pleasures. If happiness lies in activity and freedom from perplexity of soul, it would have been hard to find a happier comradeship.

Tommy and I were exactly contemporary, but I was far below his dazzling altitude. When I became a member of Vincent's he was already president of that club, and beyond doubt the most conspicuous figure of our academic generation. Indeed, I think that if at any time during our four years' residence a poll had been taken for the most popular man in the University he would have headed it. It was not only that he was a "Blue" and an assured "International"; it was far more that he was Tommy Nelson.

When I came to know him well he was living out of college in rooms in the High Street. There was generally a hansom waiting outside his door, in case it might be wanted, for he was no economist in small things. We were associated in the revival of the Caledonian Club, of which he was president and I secretary—a light-hearted institution whose members wore a marvellous uniform of green cloth and claret-coloured silk (supposed to represent the colours of the Scots thistle), and were very particular as to the Scottish ancestry—

for at least two generations on both sides – of candidates for election. An English Club, projected on the same lines, failed because only two men could be found to pass the test! The Caledonian Club dined during the winter terms with an immense parade of pipers, haggises, Atholl brose and rare clarets, and in summer gave a ladies' concert and a river picnic. This last festivity I only once attended. There were three steamers and nearly three hundred guests, and the outfit returned just before daybreak. As the enterprise stood in our name, Tommy and I had lengthy and painful explanations with the Proctors.

It is often said that it is the playtime at Oxford which is most vividly remembered – the thrill of matches and races, the hilarious dinners, the jogging back in the winter twilight from a day with hounds, the surreptitious coach to Ascot, the shining idle noons of summer time. That may be true, for no place is so nobly staged for holiday. But there were always some among us who had a touch of aloofness from the ordinary revels. Tommy had the universal popularity of Ernest Balfour – that member of his own college who had been his inseparable friend from early boyhood, and whose death in his third year was the most solemn event of our Oxford days; but he had never Ernest's bubbling, bewildering high spirits. He never gave himself wholeheartedly to exuberance. I can see him at our meetings, smiling, kindly, always a little critical. There was something in his eyes which was serious without being grave. He had a core of whinstone commonsense which he was not ashamed of, and every one of us felt that here was a man whose counsel was worth seeking. I remember that, during my last year, I had to face a very unpleasant crisis in my own college, in which, for what seemed to me good reasons, I had to take a course which brought me into violent public conflict with the majority of my contemporaries. I had most unwillingly to play a part which might be construed as priggish. I went to Tommy for advice and got the best. He, the most popular undergraduate in the University, was prepared to back me through thick and thin. The moral courage of the ordinary young man is small, and I had a full share of the youthful dislike to going against a prevailing fashion. That Tommy should be prepared to join me in the business was a comfort beyond words, and it gave me some understanding of his sturdy independence of soul.

I have said that he had an acute critical faculty and was not easily carried away. But this criticism was never used on his friends. He hated meanness and cowardice, and was incapable of either, but he would judge no man. I never heard him say an ill-natured thing. I have rarely heard him say even a severe thing. He had ever some pity for the erring, some excuse which he would not have used for himself. Following on Oxford there are always some tragedies. Brilliant, open-handed men slip into dark morasses from which they sometimes never emerge. I know of more than one case where it was Tommy's hand that pulled the

7

straggler back to the road, and no one but the straggler ever knew of it.

After Oxford for several years we drifted apart. Tommy went north to take his share in the family business in Edinburgh and look after his Argyll-shire property. I went to London to the Bar, and then for two years to South Africa. When I came back at the end of 1903 I found that Tommy had married Ernest Balfour's sister, and had settled down to the profession of publisher. I was little in Scotland in those years and we did not meet again till the autumn of 1906. Then suddenly one morning he came to see me in the Temple, and asked me to become a partner in his firm. I agreed, and after that till the end of his life we were most intimately associated.

I remember thinking how little he had changed since Oxford, except that his hair, after the fashion of his family, was becoming grizzled. He always looked amazingly fit, with a clear brown skin, and the untroubled eyes of a boy. I never saw him haggard, except at the Front. To find him at his best and happiest he had to be sought at Achna-cloich in the holiday seasons. I have never known a more assiduous sportsman. Games, indeed, he no longer cared much for, but in all wild sports he was an adept. He was a fine shot with gun and rifle, though in later years he rather lost interest in shooting and preferred other things. He was a bold rider to hounds, and used to lease a place in the Borders during the hunting season. But fish-ing, which has a trick of ousting other tastes and

8

reigning supreme, was his chief hobby. He threw an uncommonly good line, and had the patience of Job with the dour salmon of the Awe. I think the attraction of angling for him was not merely the delicate art of it, but the way in which an angler must soak himself in the genial silences of nature. Tommy was the last man to theorize about his tastes, but it was easy to read them. He had something very elemental about him. He was a great sportsman, not merely because he did everything well and with immense gusto, but because he had in his bones the love of wild life and adventure and contest.

He was an ideal Scots laird, too, in other ways. From the start he was a keen Yeomanry officer and took pains with his own training and that of his men. He was a pioneer of afforestation, and had Sir Walter Scott's ambition to make trees grow where none grew before. Above all he made landlordship an honest and worthy human relation. He looked upon all classes of men with infinite friendliness and understanding, and some response was wrung from the most angular. It was a case of liking at the first encounter, respect at the second, and a steady growth of each ever after. He had that strange power of endearing himself to people which women possess often and men rarely, without any effort on his part, without any of the easy insincerities of the conventional " good-fellow," simply by being himself and warming the atmosphere round him with his presence.

For a hundred people who knew Tommy as a

9

sportsman and a Highland laird, a dozen, maybe, knew him on his more serious sides. That was because he was shy of self-revelation and shunned any kind of parade. Yet sport bulked little in his real life, and, as he grew older, he found the man who was a sportsman and nothing more a little wearisome. The truth is that for all his abounding zest for everything he had rather a grave reflective mind, natural in one who always kept so fine a mental balance; and as time went on this seriousness grew. He had a quick sympathy and a very tender heart in face of

> the fierce confederate storm
> Of sorrow, barricadoed evermore
> Within the walls of cities.

His head was always filled with schemes of social betterment, first for his workpeople and then for the world at large. He believed profoundly in the plain man, longed for him to come to his own, and hated (if he was capable of hate) all snobbishness, brutality, and injustice. And at the same time he never fell victim to the fallacy of thinking that happiness only belonged to one way of life, and that all others must be pathological conditions. He had a robust understanding of the cheerfulness and sanity in the lives of those whom philanthropists call "the poor." Yet he was very shy of talking about his views, for he had a horror of anything like rhetoric and grandiosity. He had reacted strongly from the evangelical atmosphere of his youth, and was chary of creeds that protested too much and of people who were at ease in Zion.

He could never forget what Carlyle has put into famous words: "It is a sad but sure truth that every time you speak of a fine purpose, especially if with eloquence and to the admiration of by-standers, there is the less chance of your ever making a fact of it in your poor life."

It was this reaction, perhaps, which gave him his distaste for party politics. I cannot imagine a better candidate for Parliament, and it used to be said that he would have been returned for any Edinburgh seat he cared to stand for. But he was as likely to become a Mormon as a politician. A political faith he had, a broad undogmatic liberalism, but he would not have been happy in any party conventicle. He called himself a Liberal, as I called myself a Tory, but I cannot remember that we ever differed on any public question. Ulster, perhaps, was an exception, for I was a fiery "covenanter," and he was bored by the very mention of the subject; but I think the reason was that he so distrusted heroics of any kind in the political game that he found pose where I found sincerity. On everything else he held the same kind of creed as Raymond Asquith and Bron Lucas and the rest of us. I used to adapt the French epigram and quote it to him as his confession of faith: "All sensible men have the same politics, but what these politics are no sensible man ever tells."

Ever since I knew him I was a witness to the steady march of his mind. The Tommy of one year was very different from the Tommy of its predecessor: he had matured like a fine wine, and

II

showed richer powers and wider interests. He was never handicapped by a lumber-room of faded knowledge, like some of us who stuck closer to our books in youth. His mind was a weapon, not a set of acquirements, and the weapon was always bright and keen. His taste in literature was most catholic; but also curiously pure and austere. He was the touchstone of a good book. I often differed from his judgements, but I do not remember a single case where I did not come round to them in the end. It was the same with other matters. His alert intelligence went to the heart of things, and even when he had no reasons to give it was wise to respect his instinct.

But to his friends these qualities were secondary and only realized in the retrospect; the primary thing was the charm of his companionship. It was a sheer delight to be with him at any time, and I fear that no words can reproduce the peculiar magnetism of Tommy Nelson for those who did not know him. Something was due to uncommon good looks; more to a slow, almost lazy, kindliness in voice and manner; much to his constant humour and sympathy; most to the generosity of soul which shone like a light in all his doings. Once, I remember, my wife and I spent a month with him alone on a Norwegian farm, pursuing salmon which that year were elusive. We dozed, read, and strolled most of the days and fished through the amber midnights. I can never forget the long talks in that big untidy room, where we lived as if in camp, and cast everything not in immediate use on the floor so that they were caught in an under-tow of disorder, and books, papers, reels, flies, pipes, and cigarettes disappeared from our ken for ever; or the sleepy afternoons among the birches of the hillside; or the walks back from the river with the sky of morning changing from sapphire to turquoise above the pines. Nor can I forget the smoking-room fire at Achnacloich, which seemed to burn with a cheerier glow than other fires; or the days in the rain on the Black Lochs or beside the dour-hearted Awe. Those hours can never be recaptured, not only because they belonged to youth which has fled, but because Tommy is gone.

And yet—and yet! Looking back I can see that I was never quite at ease about him. He was the properest piece of manhood I have ever known, the sanest, the wisest, the kindest, the type to which every man hopes that his sons may some day attain. But I felt that he was fitted for greater things than any I could foresee for him. About some people one has that consciousness of powers too big for their environment. A life of great domestic happiness, innumerable friends, a world enlivened and comforted by his presence — it might seem enough for most men, but it seemed too little for Tommy. For he was the stuff of which adventurers are made, and where was the chance of adventure in our cushioned world?

Then came the War and the old life passed away in a night. We were back in an elemental region of death and hazard and sacrifice, where fortitude was to be tested in the ancient way.

13

TOMMY NELSON

From the first hour Tommy's one thought was to give all he possessed to his country's service. He esteemed everyone but himself, admired greatly his fellow-soldiers, and was modestly eager to make himself worthy of them. But from the beginning he was a fine soldier, by virtue of his quick intelligence, his unshakeable good humour, his faithfulness, and his great courage. He and I used often to talk about courage, and his view was that every healthy man had a large stock of the physical sort. He had, beyond doubt, and it was the best kind, for he knew what fear meant but would never know how to yield to it.

The early months were a difficult time. He at once rejoined his Yeomanry, the Lothians and Border Horse, and trained with them at home till September 1915, fretting at his inaction, while his brother Ian was in every battle from Neuve Chapelle to Loos. Just after Loos he went to France, and his squadron was attached to the 25th Division as divisional cavalry. Early in 1916 he had several spells of staff work, and in May became observation officer for the 50th Division in the Kemmel district. In August he went south to the Somme as observation officer for the 5th Corps, and in that unhallowed place he and I foregathered. I had not seen him for more than a year.

That drizzling autumn in Picardy is still a nightmare to remember, though I had an easy job compared with most people. Perhaps it was because I was ill, and liable to retire at any moment to a bed in a casualty clearing station. The smell of

14

an incinerator will always bring back to me long tramps in wet trenches, a downfall of cold rain, and a bleak sense of futility. When I met Tommy I discovered that he too was depressed. One October afternoon I found myself in his corps' area, so I borrowed a car and set off to look for him. By chance I met him on the road, sitting on the back of a motor-lorry, and we spent the rest of the day together.

I noticed that he had suddenly grown very haggard and more silent than before. It is no light job for a man of over forty to be pitchforked into war, and Tommy's work was peculiarly wearing. He had a number of observation posts to look after, and as the corps headquarters were miles from the line, he had constant journeys to make by any means of transport he could find – oftenest, perhaps, on foot. He had no kind of home anywhere, and spent his time on the roads or in shell-holes and dug-outs, wherever night happened to overtake him. It was a lonely life and more comfortless than that of most front-line trenches. The work, too, was difficult and harassing and, of course, very risky. Tommy did it uncommonly well, for he had a stalker's eye for country and a closely reasoning mind. But the strain was wearing him down.

Things changed when in November his corps became engaged in a great battle. He was in the thick of the action at Beaucourt, and sent back the first clear account of the position on the morning of the second day. In December he rejoined his regiment at Marieux – for Picardy a comparatively

pleasant habitation - and in January 1917 he came
home on leave. By that time he had wholly recovered his spirits and bodily fitness, and when he
came to see me in London I was delighted at the
revival of the old Tommy. He was by way of changing to more congenial work, and on my advice had
applied for the Tanks service, the Flying Corps
being impossible on the ground of age. In February
he was once again in the line, and did admirable
work during the following up of the German retreat, for which he was recommended for a D.S.O.
Then early in March he joined Tanks H.Q. as
intelligence officer under my friend Captain Hotblack.

I am glad to think that the last weeks of his life
were the happiest he spent during the campaign.
The Tanks service was a real corps d'élite, the
keenest and ablest young man, perhaps, in the
whole British army. Certainly I have never been
in better company than in Hugh Elles's little mess
at Bermicourt. Tommy greatly admired and loved
them all, and he loved, too, the novel science of the
thing and its boundless possibilities. He was as
keen about it in his letters to me as he had ever
been to go fishing on a spring morning. As the hour
of the great movement at Arras drew near, the
Tank Corps were busy, for it was recognized that
it was to be a field day for them. Very early on the
morning of Monday, 9 April, about the time when
Alastair was leading his Scots Fusiliers over the
parapets half a mile farther north, Tommy was
standing with Captain Hotblack in a trench a little

east of the railway station. He was not to live to see his tanks take the Railway Triangle and go through the Harp as through blotting paper. A shell fell between him and Hotblack, wounding his friend severely and bringing to him instantaneous death.

He was buried in a little cemetery formed out of a piece of open ground behind the station, and ten days later after much searching I found his grave. His boyishness had all come back to him in those last days.

> Far other is that battle in the West
> Whereto we move, than when we strove in youth;

but I know that he carried to that last fight the same happy ardour which he had kept undimmed from childhood.

His death left an aching sense of bereavement in a great multitude not only of friends but of slight and casual acquaintances. He had his roots so deep and far spread that his loss made a bigger hole in the life of Scotland than would have been the case, perhaps, with any other man of his years. Heu! quanto minus est cum reliquis versari quam tui meminisse! Good fortune, of which he had an ample share, could not spoil him or weaken his fibre for the great test of manhood which he had to face in the end. He was a rare being just because he was so superbly normal, so wholly in tune with ordinary humanity, and therefore most fitted to help in the "difficult but not desperate life of man." In the case of others we might regret the premature loss to the world of

17

some peculiar talent; with Tommy we mourned especially the loss of a talent for living worthily and for helping others to do likewise. It is the kind of loss least easy to forget, and yet one which comes to be contemplated without pain. He had succeeded most fully in life, for he crowded his days with honourable activities and made his world immeasurably the better for his presence. The influence of that wise and tender and happy spirit will fructify in the lives of many of us long after the war has become only a memory: for what we loved best in Tommy was that part of him which cannot die.

II

BRON LUCAS

AUBERON THOMAS HERBERT was born in 1876, the son of the Hon. Auberon Herbert by his marriage with the sister of the last Earl Cowper. He was educated at Bedford Grammar School and Balliol. At Oxford he rowed 7 in the University Boat in 1898 and 1899. He went through the South African War as "Times" correspondent, and received a wound which compelled the amputation of a leg. In 1905 he succeeded his uncle, Lord Cowper, in the baronies of Lucas and Dingwall. He became private secretary to Mr. Haldane at the War Office in 1907, and in 1908 Under-Secretary for War. In 1911 he was Under-Secretary for the Colonies, and later in the year Parliamentary Secretary to the Board of Agriculture. In 1914 he entered the Cabinet as President of the Board of Agriculture. In 1915 he joined the Royal Flying Corps, obtained his pilot's certificate, and saw much service in Egypt. After some time at home as an instructor, he went to France during the battle of the Somme, and was shot down over the enemy lines on 10 November 1916.

BRON LUCAS

I HAVE known a fair number of gipsies in my life, often in most unfitting professions. Sometimes fate was kind to them and gave them scope for vagrancy; pencilled scrawls with odd outlandish postmarks were all we heard of them; and once in a blue moon they would turn up with brown faces and far-regarding eyes to tantalise us homekeepers with visions of the unattainable. Oftener their gipsyhood was repressed, and only the old fret in spring told where their thoughts lay. But I have never known a more whole-hearted, hard-bitten nomad than Bron. Nomad, indeed, is not the word, for he did not crave travel and change; a Hampshire meadow gave him all he wanted. But he was a gipsy to the core of his being, a creature of the wayside camp, wood smoke and the smell of earth. Some very ancient forbear was re-born in him; as in his cousin Julian Grenfell, who wrote of himself as one "who every year has an increasing desire to live in a blanket under a bush, and will soon get bored with the bush and the blanket."

At Oxford he was the link of his Balliol set with the world of sport; for his perfect physique made him a great athlete, and he rowed for his last two years in the University boat. At that time Balliol rowing was not yet the famous thing it became a little later, and to have a man in the Oxford boat

21

was a novelty for the college. But Bron had uncommonly little of the ordinary sportsman about him, being, as I have said, a gipsy. Far better than the ritual of games he loved his own private adventures in by-ways of the countryside. He had an astonishing knowledge of birds and beasts and all wild things. Most of his friends were fine scholars, but he did not essay the thorny path of academic honours, having better things to think about. We were all lovers of poetry and contemners of music. Bron loved poetry, but he had also a passion for music. I once induced him to make a speech in the Union; but after an excellent beginning he grew bored and, like the late Duke of Devonshire, stopped in the middle of a sentence. For politics he cared not at all. He was most pleasant to look at, and most gentle and courteous in manner, but his petulant mouth and great wondering eyes gave him a changeling air, as of one a little puzzled by life. He was like some wild thing tamed and habituated to a garden, but still remembering "the bright speed it bore in its high mountain cradle."

On the outbreak of war in 1899 he was off at once to South Africa, taking the first chance he got, which was that of "Times" correspondent. There he was abundantly happy. He was not specially interested in military affairs, but he loved the spacious land and the adventurous life. His letters to me at the time were one long chant of praise. "When I think of the dull things I was doing last year," he wrote, "I am simply staggered at the luck that has brought me here." Presently, advancing too far forward in an action (for those were the days when the trade of war correspondent was still an adventure) he got a rifle bullet in his foot. The wound was badly mismanaged, and when he came back to England his leg had to be amputated below the knee.

To a man of his tastes such a loss might well have been crippling. To Bron it simply did not matter at all. He behaved as if nothing had happened, and went on with the life he loved. It cannot have been an easy job, but he never showed the strain of it. He was just as fine a sportsman as before, and his high spirits were, if anything, more infectious. During the later stages of his convalescence I used to stay with him at his uncle's house of Panshanger, and catch trout with the dry fly in the Mimram. He was a wonderful fisherman, but that gentle art was only one of his accomplishments. Soon he was scampering about in the New Forest, and hunting, and playing tennis, and stalking on some of the roughest hills of Scotland. He must have had bad hours, but he held his head high to the world and his friends. He was not going to be depressed even for a moment by a small thing like the loss of a leg.

When I came back from South Africa in 1903 I found that Bron had become, under Raymond Asquith's guidance, a Liberal candidate for Parliament, and was making speeches about Free Trade. At Oxford he had been, like me, a Tory and a member of the Canning Club; but that excellent society was not bigoted, for I remember that at two successive meetings, after drinking the toast of Church and State, we disestablished the Church and nationalized the land of England. I cannot believe that then he had any very serious politics, for in 1904 he and I spent a week-end together at the Hautboy Inn in Surrey, and his views on foreign affairs were rampantly Bismarckian. He wanted something with which to fill his time, for he was living under the shadow of succession to a peerage and large estates.

His uncle, the last Lord Cowper, died in the summer of 1905, and Bron became Lord Lucas and the owner of several great houses. He got them off his hands as fast as he could, for the only place he cared for was his home at Picket Post in the New Forest. A lesser man might have been oppressed by his possessions, but Bron was too unworldly to feel any oppression. They mattered nothing in his scheme of life. For he was still the gipsy, careless of a sedentary world, and with all the belongings he needed in his wallet.

Then there befell him the most fantastic fate. In 1906 a Liberal Government came into power, and Bron, as one of the few Liberal peers, was marked down for preferment. He became Mr. Haldane's private secretary at the War Office. In 1908 he was Under-Secretary for War, and rebutting in the House of Lords Lord Roberts' plea for national service. He was not a good speaker, but his boyish charm and gallantry pleased people, and even his opponents wished him well. In 1911 he was for a short time Under-Secretary for the Colonies. That same year he went as Parliamentary Secretary to the Board of Agriculture, where he was a real success, for he was a true countryman, knowing at first hand what most politicians are only told. In 1914 he entered the Cabinet as President of the Board of Agriculture, and held the office till the formation of the Coalition in May 1915, when he most thankfully laid it down.

Was there ever an odder destiny for a gipsy than to be a Cabinet Minister in spite of himself at thirty-eight? No man could have wanted it less. He did his work well – the agricultural part extraordinarily well – but his heart was never in it. He had no ambition, and the long round of conferences, deputations, unmeaning speeches, idle debates, was wholly distasteful. He disliked London, shunned ordinary society, and was happy only in the company of his friends. At a ball, when by any rare chance he attended one, he had the air of a hunted stag. To see him at a party was to get some idea of how Marius looked among the ruins of Carthage. But at Picket or in Scotland, shooting, hunting, fishing, or bird-watching, he was the old Bron again, with the old zest and simplicity. When I met him in London in those days I used to think that he looked more puzzled than ever. He seemed to find the world rather tarnished and dusty, and to be longing for a clearer air.

When he left the Cabinet in 1915 he found what he had been seeking. Though he was many years over the age, he managed to join the Royal Flying

Corps and trained for his pilot's certificate. Here his wonderful eye and nerve stood him in good stead, and presently he became a most competent pilot. He was sent out to Egypt, whence stories came back to us of strange adventures - crashing in the desert many miles from help, and such like. He was back in England in the spring of 1916, engaged in instructing recruits, and more than once came very near death. But Bron had risked his neck all his days, and his friends hoped that his standing luck might carry him through.

In May of that year to my surprise I found him at a party - almost the last given by Count Benckendorff at the Russian Embassy. He asked me if I thought that the old political game would ever start again. "If it does," he said, "it will start without me." He was a picture of weatherbeaten health, but I noticed that his eyes were different. They had become more deeply set, as happens to airmen, and also they had lost their puzzled look. He had found something for which he had long been seeking. Up in the clouds he had come to his own and discovered the secret of life. He never spoke of it, for he was as shy and elusive in these things as a young girl, but it could be read in his eyes.

It had always been his desire to serve on the Western front, and he went there half-way through the Battle of the Somme. I am glad to think that I saw something of him during his last weeks on earth. His camp was beside the road from Amiens to Doullens: his friend Maurice Baring was at the R.F.C. Headquarters, and I was at General Headquarters at Beauquesne; so we were all three only a few miles from each other. The concluding days of October and the first week of November were full of strong gales from the south-west, which gravely hampered our flying, for our machines were drifted too far over the enemy lines and had to fight their way back slowly against a head wind. It was an eery season on the bleak Picardy downs, scourged and winnowed by blasts, with the noise of the guns from the front line coming fitfully in the pauses like the swell of breakers on a coast. One evening, I remember, I rode over to have tea with Bron, when the west was crimson with sunset and above me huge clouds were scudding before the gale. They were for the most part ragged and tawny, like wild horses, but before them went a white horse, the leader of the unearthly cavalry. It seemed to me that I was looking at a ride of Valkyries, the Shield Maids of Odin hasting eastward to the battle front to choose the dead for Valhalla.

Two days later Maurice came to me and told me that Bron was missing. The chances were about equal that he was a prisoner, and for days we dared to hope. Then, early in December, we heard that he was dead. When our troops advanced to victory in the autumn of 1918 they found his grave.

There could be no sorrow in such a death, though for his friends an undying regret. The homely English countryside, the return of Spring, the sports which he loved are the emptier for his absence. Maurice Baring has written of this in his beautiful elegy.

> So when the Spring of the world shall shrive our stain,
> After the winter of war,
> When the poor world awakes to peace once more,
> After such night of ravage and of rain,
> You shall not come again.
> You shall not come to taste the old Spring weather,
> To gallop through the soft untrampled heather,
> To bathe and bake your body on the grass.
> We shall be there. Alas!
> But not with you. When Spring shall wake the earth,
> And quicken the scarred fields to the new birth,
> Our grief shall grow. For what can Spring renew
> More fiercely for us than the need of you?

But Bron had been gathered into these things, for he belonged to them. No man ever more completely found himself. He was not quite of this world; or, rather, he was of that earlier fairer world that our civilization has so grossly overlaid. He lived close to the kindly earth, and then he discovered the kindlier air, and that pure exultant joy of living which he had always sought. "In the hot fit of life" – the words are Stevenson's – "a-tiptoe on the highest point of being, he passes at a bound on to the other side. The noise of the mallet and chisel is scarcely quenched, the trumpets are hardly done blowing, when, trailing with him clouds of glory, the happy-starred, full-blooded spirit shoots into the spiritual land." But he had never been very far from it. Death to him was less a setting forth than a returning. On that wild autumn morning Bron did not fly away; he came home.

28

III
CECIL RAWLING

CECIL RAWLING was born in 1870 and educated at Clifton College. He obtained his first commission in the Somerset Light Infantry, and as a young officer went through the North-West Frontier Campaign of 1897-8. He was in the Tibetan Expedition of 1904, and immediately thereafter led an exploring party into Southern Tibet, which determined for the first time the sources of the Bramaputra. For this work he received the thanks of the Government of India and the C.I.E. His next expedition was to Dutch New Guinea in 1909-11, where his party discovered a new pigmy race. At the outbreak of war he took command of one of the new battalions of his old regiment, and went with it to France in the spring of 1915. He was in the Hooge fighting of July-August 1915, and spent that winter in the Ypres Salient. He was given command of the 62nd Infantry Brigade (and a C.M.G.) just before the First Battle of the Somme, and his brigade, which was in the 21st Division, played a great part in that action. During 1917 he was engaged in the fighting for the Siegfried Line, and later in the Third Battle of Ypres. He was killed on 23 October of that year by a stray shell outside his headquarters near Hooge.

CECIL RAWLING

AMONG the many things which are now gone out of the world is the old British Regular Army. The historian of the future will speculate on the character of that wonderful force, which a German military critic has called "a perfect thing apart," and will do justice to those latter-day Spartans who stood their ground in a more fateful Thermopylae.

> Their shoulders held the heavens suspended,
> They stood, and earth's foundations stay,
> What God abandoned these defended,
> And saved the sum of things for pay.

One fact is worth putting on record now before it is forgotten, and that is the curious likeness among the "Old Contemptibles" between officers and men. I refer especially to the officers of the line regiments, and more particularly perhaps to the light infantry regiments. Below all the differences of birth and education there was a common temperament – a kind of humorous realism about life, a dislike of tall talk, a belief in inherited tradition and historic ritual, a rough and ready justness, a deep cheerfulness which was not inconsistent with a surface pessimism. And of all the regular officers I have known Cecil Rawling was most akin to the best type of British private soldier. He generally

31

took a dark view of the immediate prospect; therefore he was never seriously depressed. He had an unshakeable confidence in the ultimate issue; therefore he never thought it worth while to mention it. He was always slightly lost; therefore he could never be completely lost, whether in Tibet or on a Flanders battlefield. That is perhaps the reason why he was so successful an explorer and so good a soldier. The man who insists on having the next stage neatly outlined before he starts will be unnerved if he cannot see his way. Cecil drove on cheerfully into the mist, because he had been there so often before and knew that somewhere on the farther side there was clear sky.

As a friend he was a legacy from my brother Willie. They had met in India, after Cecil came back from his Tibetan expedition, and, since Willie had the same passion for mountains and strange lands and was always prowling about the northern frontiers, the two became close friends. They undertook a history of Tibet together, in which the one was to furnish the historical and the other the linguistic and topographical knowledge. When Willie stayed with us in London during his leave in 1909 Cecil was a constant visitor. He was on the eve of departing for New Guinea, and I remember thinking how casual was this eminent traveller. I was utterly wrong; Cecil was a most cool and patient planner of expeditions; but his gentleness and simplicity left the impression of a delightful boy who does everything "for fun."

In 1912 he was back in England, and in the summer

CECIL RAWLING

Willie came home to die. During that awful November, when the noblest spirit I have ever known faced uncomplainingly the end of youth and hope, Cecil came to see me and wept like a child. Like Nelson, his was too great a heart to be ashamed of tears.

After that we became very intimate friends. When he was in Somerset with his regiment he used to come and see us on every visit to town, and we would sit long into the night talking about far countries. He was so modest that no one could have guessed from his talk the remarkable things he had done. Already he was in the front rank of the younger explorers. He had discovered the sources of the Bramaputra, thereby forestalling Sven Hedin. In Dutch New Guinea he had undergone hardships which it would be hard to parallel from any modern expedition. In that land of swamps and fever and flies and breathless heat his party had lived for months without any of the ordinary traveller's comforts, for their supplies were the stores left over from Shackleton's South Pole Expedition. Imagine the joys of eating under a tropical sun food selected for life in the Antarctic! They had failed to climb Carstensz, but had discovered a new pigmy race, and had added greatly to our knowledge of the fauna and flora of that unpleasant isle. Cecil, after his fashion, made light of the discomforts, and you will find few complaints in his excellent book on the subject; but the business must have been one long purgatory. Yet he was eager to set off on some new errand. Exploration was the thing that lay nearest to his heart, and I think that the greatest pleasure of his life was the award to him in 1916 of the Royal Geographical Society's Founder's Medal.

His interest in travel was mainly the finding out of something unknown before; mine was the climbing of high mountains; and early in 1914 he conceived a venture in which we could join hands. This was nothing less than the first ascent of Mount Everest. The view he had had of that mountain from the Tibetan plateau in 1904 had convinced him that it might be climbed from that side. He now became a thorough-going Alpinist, and for the first time – since the object of ascending Carstensz had been exploration rather than climbing – he acquired a passion for the mere getting to the top of peaks. Through the spring and summer of 1914 he and I were very busy obtaining permission from the various Governments concerned. He had planned a most elaborate expedition to work during two seasons. The first year was to be devoted to prospecting the north side of Everest, and exploring the possibilities of a high camp to be used as a base for the final effort. The thing might prove impossible; but, if not, in the second season a strong party was to make a push for the summit. We arranged for every kind of scientist to accompany us, and we had provisionally selected our Swiss guides. Members of Cecil's old Tibetan parties would be available in India. The thought of being the first to set foot on the highest point on the globe went to our heads, and, though I had many other

34

duties, I hoped to combine the expedition with some business in India, and had arranged to join Cecil for the second season.

The War put an end to these pleasant dreams, and Cecil was snatched away to his proper task of soldiering. He had no special taste for it, though he had fought in Indian frontier wars, for his mind had become absorbed in exploration; and he felt much as a lawyer might feel who, having held Cabinet office, is compelled to go back to his prac- tice at the bar. He was given command of one of the new Service battalions of his regiment, the Somerset Light Infantry, and trained with them at Bordon Camp. I remember that he came to see me in October in a mood of dire depression. At that time the Government looked forward to a short war, and Lord Kitchener was considered a pessi- mist for talking about three years. Cecil lifted up his voice and prophesied. The war, he said, would last every bit of four years, if we meant to win. Russia would not last out the course-he knew Russia. Like the British sailor of Nelson's day he had little respect for any Continentals, and he was not prepared to pin his faith to France. The war would be won in the fourth year by the British and the Americans. No, not by the British Fleet; by the British Army, which by that time would have grown to be the best in the world. It is worth re- cording this prophecy by an old regular officer, for at the time I thought it mad.

He wanted to have Alastair in his battalion, but Alastair had resolved to go to a Scottish regiment. The next I heard of Cecil he was in France with the 14th Light Division, and in the thick of the Hooge affair at the end of July 1915. For the better part of a year he was in the Ypres area, and even the memories of the New Guinea swamps paled before that place of mud and misery. Looking back, I am inclined to think that the sufferings of the battalions who were perpetually in and about Ypres during the winter of 1915-16 were as bad as anything in the campaign. Cecil on his return home preferred not to discuss the subject. Once we proposed to take him to a "murder" play, which was then the talk of London. He begged to be excused. After a year in the Ypres Salient, he said, he was inclined to be b l a s é about murders.

He was unconscionably long in getting promotion, considering the very general respect in which his fighting qualities were held. It was just before the Battle of the Somme that he was given command of the 62nd Infantry Brigade in the 21st Division, which was now under David Campbell. I saw that division at Loos in 1915 in sore tribulation; but throughout the rest of the campaign it never looked back. At the Somme it took Fricourt and Mametz Wood and Bazentin le Petit Wood, and crowned its glorious record by the capture of Gueudecourt on 26 September. It is no light business for an enemy to meet a British division which has a score to wipe off. On the first day of the action I tried to get through to Cecil, but Mametz village had not fallen and I blundered into the German machine guns. Repeatedly during the battle I made the same attempt, but his brigade had a trick of being always hotly engaged when I tried to visit it. The result was that we never met in France.

We corresponded regularly, and he sent me most admirable accounts of his different fights. He was becoming a very keen soldier, and was on the high road to a division. By men and officers alike he was adored. He was intrepid, if duty called for intrepidity, but he had no liking for useless bravado. His brigade was his first care, and he husbanded it as a wise traveller husbands his failing supplies. There is nothing that men appreciate more than the knowledge that their commander values their lives and will not needlessly sacrifice them. At the same time he played the game of war in its full rigour. He hated to be accused of gallantry. He was a timid man, he said, who preferred to go round a wall rather than butt against it, who didn't like shells, and who intended before the next war to go into the Church. That is the traditional pose of the British regular. Cecil feared very little on earth, except the reputation of a hero.

He was Billy's godfather, and when he came home used to pay his respects to that truculent godchild. On these visits he never seemed war-weary. His strong brown face and kind eyes, his rapid speech, his ready laugh, were the same as ever. I never felt about him - as I felt about certain others - that he would not see Peace. He was so solid and competent, with such a grip on life and on himself, that I believed he would weather the war and that he and I might yet scramble among the Himalayas. Then came the long tragedy of Third Ypres, and I had from him full accounts of the doings of his brigade. In October of that year the main operations were nearly at an end, and I looked any day to see Cecil home again. He must soon get his division, and, when all is said, a divisional-general's task is less risky than a brigadier's.

Suddenly I had a message from his brother that Cecil was dead. On the 23rd of October, while he was talking with some of his officers outside his brigade headquarters at Hooge, a stray shell fell among them and killed him instantaneously. He was then in his forty-seventh year.

Of all the friends of whom I have written in this little book he was the one whom my children knew best. He played with them like one of themselves, for he had that happy childlikeness which belongs to the pure in heart. I am glad that they should have known a member of that great company, the old British regulars. He had crowded into a short career more of honourable activity and true success and sincere friendship than is achieved by most men who reach the allotted span. His passion was for high places, and in the long endurance of the war he scaled greater heights than Everest. After five years' separation he has joined Willie again, and, since such generous ardour cannot end with death, I think of them as comrades now in the high enterprises of immortal spirits.

IV

BASIL BLACKWOOD

BASIL TEMPLE BLACKWOOD was born in 1870, the third son of the first Marquis of Dufferin, who was Governor General of Canada, Viceroy of India, and British Ambassador at Paris. He was educated at Harrow and at Balliol College, Oxford. After much travelling he served as Deputy Judge Advocate in the South African War, then on Lord Milner's staff, and then for five years as Assistant Colonial Secretary in the Orange River Colony. In 1907 he went to Barbados as Colonial Secretary, and returned to London in 1909, where he held various official posts. At the outbreak of war he was attached to the 9th Lancers, and was severely wounded at Messines. During his slow convalescence he acted as Private Secretary to the Lord Lieutenant in Ireland. In the summer of 1916 he obtained a commission in the Grenadier Guards, and was killed in a night raid in the Ypres area on 3 July 1917.

BASIL BLACKWOOD

AT Oxford the doings of Basil Blackwood were a legend handed down from the generation that preceded ours - the generation of Hubert Howard and Alfred Grant. Hilaire Belloc, who belonged to that epoch and was still up with us, spoke of him so often that his name became as familiar as one of our contemporaries. We knew him, too, from the delightful drawings with which he illustrated "The Bad Child's Book of Beasts." But in those days he was so much out of England on hunting trips and other ventures, that I did not meet him till I found him as a colleague on Lord Milner's staff in South Africa.

He was precisely such a figure as I had expected from his reputation. I remember him as he first appeared in that ugly office in Johannesburg, where we occupied adjacent rooms. Slight in build, with a beautifully shaped head and soft dark sleepy eyes, everything about him - voice, manner, frame - was fine and delicate. His air was full always of a quiet cheerfulness, with a suggestion of devilment in the background, as if he were only playing at decorum. His interest in life was unquenchable, and he found endless amusements in that somewhat dull environment. I can see him with his dog Gyp, walking with his light foot on the dusty red roads; or cantering among the blue gums, for he was never long out of the saddle.

BASIL BLACKWOOD

With his pointed face and neat black moustache he had the air of a Spanish hidalgo, and there was always about him a certain silken foreign grace. Once I saw the hidalgo capering down the road on an elegant mule, but a mule's shoulders are precarious things, and the next I saw was that the rider and saddle had gone over the beast's head into the dust.

We were a pleasant company in those days—Billy Lambton, Hugh Wyndham, Gerard Sellar, Guy Brooke, and Geoffrey Dawson—but it was Basil who introduced the fantastic element that kept us all from the usual ennui of a staff. His serene good temper was unshakeable, and I do not think he was ever bored in his life. Long after most of us had returned he stayed on in South Africa, and was happy even in Bloemfontein, which I regard as the dreariest of habitations. He had the expectant mood, and was always waiting for some chance of adventure to turn up. His official work was most competently done, though he had some difficulty in restraining his propensity to make fun of things. He used to draft despatches for Lord Milner to sign, and I remember one which began "With reference to my able despatch of such and such a date"—an opening which, had it been sent in that form, would have considerably startled the Colonial Office.

He was always drawing in that brilliant manner he had discovered for himself, for he had never been taught by anybody. I remember hundreds of sketches, some of which I possess, admirable in

wit and bold draughtsmanship. He used to illustrate despatches for our private edification. One,
I remember, contained the information that "The
Land Board is empowered to make advances to
settlers." Basil drew a wonderful picture of a gross
and sentimental Land Board "making advances"
to a coy settler. He and I projected a "Child's History of South Africa," for which he was to do the
drawings and I the verses. The work had perforce
to stop, having become too scandalous. My rhymes
were bad enough, but Basil's pictures of Dingaan's
Day, of Slagter's Nek, of the doings of Miss Emily
Hobhouse, and of some of the Semitic kings of the
Rand were an outrage.

Most of us returned from South Africa to our
different professions, but Basil scorned his proper
calling of the law, and preferred a life of interest to
the orthodox career of success. After the Orange
River Colony he went for two years to Barbados.
There he began to pine for London and his friends,
and returned to what seemed the most unsuitable
work of the new Labour Exchanges. After that he
became Assistant Secretary to the Development
Commission, where he was more in place. The
truth is he was not the kind of man who fits easily
into a groove. He was too versatile, too much in
love with the coloured aspects of life, and too careless of worldly wisdom. For one occupation, indeed, he had the highest talent. Not for nothing
was he his father's son. He had an hereditary instinct for administration and diplomacy, and his
great gift of winning popularity, his charm of man-

ner, his fine sense of atmosphere, his imagination and his very real love of his fellow creatures would have made him the best of colonial governors. He should have begun at the top, for he was better fitted for that than for any intermediate stage. I used to think it a thousand pities that he had not been born a peer with great possessions. There is never much area of choice for our governors and viceroys, but they must begin from a certain platform, and, had Basil had the platform, he might well have repeated his father's career.

In one thing he was wholly successful. He was the most cherished and welcome of friends. Wherever he appeared he brought a warmth and colour into the air. It is difficult to describe the fascination of his company, because it depended on so many subtle things - a peculiar grace and gentleness of manner; a perpetual expectation, as if the world was enormously bigger and more interesting than people thought; a suspicion, too, of devil-may-careness, which made havoc of weary partition walls. Without any noise or extravagance he seemed to oxygenate the atmosphere around him. He was an incomparable letter-writer, the best I have ever known except Raymond Asquith, and he had the extra advantage of being able to illustrate his epistles. Alas! I doubt if, any more than Raymond's, those delectable letters can ever be published.

The first hint of war was, of course, to him what the first waft of scent is to a pack of hounds. He was off like an arrow on the old search for adven-

44

ture. To most of us the war was the wrecking of cherished shelters; to Basil it was the breaking down of barriers. He was given a commission in the Intelligence Corps and was fortunate enough to get attached to the 9th Lancers, who were all his friends. With that great regiment he went to France in the early August of 1914.

The story of the 9th during the first month of war may be read in Francis Grenfell's diaries and letters - the misery of cavalry cramped among the wire and railway embankments and pit-heads of Mons; the notable work of De Lisle's 2nd Brigade in protecting the right flank of Sir Charles Fergusson's 5th Division, when Francis won the Victoria Cross. Thereafter Francis went off the scene with a bullet in his thigh, and the 9th Lancers started on the great retreat. Basil was with them then; with them he shared in the advance at the Marne and saw the beginning of the long war of trenches on the Aisne. I am sure that in those days he was perfectly happy, for he had his friends around him, a horse between his legs, and before him all the unmapped possibilities of war. When Francis's diaries begin again the brigade was in Flanders and Basil was galloping for the General. They fought their way by Merris to Ploegsteert and Le Gheir, and in the last days of October took part in Allenby's defence of the Messines ridge - not the least desperate part of the great struggle of First Ypres. On 31 October, it will be remembered, after a heavy shelling the enemy forced our thin lines out of Messines. We hear of Basil moving about in all parts of the field on that wild day, keeping up some link between the command and Francis's handful of lancers in the trenches east of the village. Both were badly wounded by shell-fire, and Francis records his delight, when he arrived at Bailleul, to find Basil on the stretcher alongside him. They were the only two officers in Messines that day who were not taken captive by the enemy.

It was a long time before Basil got well again. He stayed in Ireland and acted as private secretary to Lord Wimborne, in which capacity he had many curious adventures during the Sinn Fein rebellion of Easter 1916. After that the Irish Government collapsed, and he was free to return to the wars. He received a commission in the Grenadier Guards and went to France early in 1917. In July the British armies were beginning to get into position for the Third Battle of Ypres, and all along the front there was a perpetual succession of raids into the enemy lines. On the night of the 3rd Basil led one of these forays and did not return. It was of a piece with the anomalies of the war that a man of such varied powers and rich experience should fall at the age of forty-six as a second-lieutenant.

It has become a fashion to talk of our dead as "new Elizabethans" and to credit all with a certain zest in the business, as a romantic adventure. Alas! some of the best had not a shadow of this feeling; to them it was only a grim sacrifice due to their manhood and their country. But of Basil the phrase may be used with truth. He was of the same breed

BASIL BLACKWOOD

as the slender gallants who singed the beard of the
king of Spain and, like Essex, tossed their plumed
hats into the sea in joy of the enterprise, or who
sold their swords to any cause which had daylight
and honour in it. His like had left their bones in
farther spaces than any race on earth, and from
their unchartered and accidental wanderings the
British Empire has been born. He did not seek to
do things so much as to see them, to be among them
and to live in the atmosphere of wonder and gay
achievement. He was not, like Bron, a gipsy, for
he was a creature of civilization, but of another
civilization than ours. If spirits return into human
shape, perhaps his once belonged to a young
grandee of the Lisbon court, who stormed with
Albuquerque the citadels of the Indies and died in
the quest for Prester John. He had the streak of
Ariel in him, and his fancy had always wings.
"For to admire and for to see" was ever his motto.
In a pedestrian world he held to the old cavalier
grace, and wherever romance called he followed
with careless gallantry.

V

JACK WORTLEY

JOHN STUART-WORTLEY was born in 1880, the only son of the late Archibald Stuart-Wortley. He was educated at Mr. Vaughan's house at Eton. At seventeen he was apprenticed to the Merchant Service, and left it in 1899 to go to South Africa as a trooper in the Hertfordshire Yeomanry. There he obtained a commission in the Scottish Horse, was wounded at Moedwill, and was twice mentioned in despatches. In 1902 he was given a commission in the Scottish Rifles and seconded to the North Nigeria Regiment, and was in charge of the transport in the Anglo-French Boundary Expedition to Lake Chad in 1903. He then went to the 11th Sudanese Regiment, and served in the Sudan with them, and later as a civil administrator, till 1912, receiving the Order of the Medjidieh. In 1912 he married and settled down in England. Early in the War he was given command of the 21st Royal Fusiliers (Public Schools Corps), and went with them to France in November 1915. In 1916 he was second in command of the 2/5th South Staffordshires (T.F.), with whom he went to France in the following year. Later he commanded the 2/6th Battalion of the same regiment. He was wounded in 1917 and was mentioned in despatches. He fell while commanding his battalion at Bullecourt on 21 March 1918.

JACK WORTLEY

JACK WORTLEY, when I first met him, reminded me of Basil Blackwood, though in most physical and mental traits they were far apart. He was the same natural adventurer, with a gift for finding himself in odd predicaments and a genius for getting out of them. Both were alike in their sangfroid, their dangerous sense of fun, and their appetite for the new and unexplored. But Basil was the eternal pilgrim whose wanderlust would not be sated till his death, while Jack had a trick of being homesick during all his travels, even when he was greatly enjoying himself and would not have returned if he could. Jack would certainly have settled down in England as a country gentleman, for he had a passion for the little things of home, and would have been as careful of his house, cellar, and gardens as if he had never been a tent-dweller. But for Basil age would not have loosed the bands of Orion.

I first met Jack in 1905, when he was home from the Sudan on leave, but I had heard of him for years before. His fantastic career was the fount of many tales in his family, and when I saw him I understood that they must all be true. He had a square head and a fine forehead, bright, mirthful, blue eyes, a Roman nose, and the rolling gait of a sailor. His upper teeth slightly projected under the eaves of his moustache and gave him a perpetual air of suppressed humour. Even when he was grave there was a hint of comedy waiting very near. Few boys can have ever had a more varied upbringing. He was at Mr. Vaughan's house at Eton, but he was not an apt scholar, and his years there were chiefly remarkable for ingenious practical jokes, which are still a tradition in the school. At seventeen it became clear that he could not stay longer at Eton, and his parents wisely decided to give him the chance of learning discipline in a stiff profession. So at seventeen he was apprenticed to the Merchant Service.

He was a born sailor and for two years was uncommonly happy. He was trained in the old four-masted clippers, and in different vessels learned all there was to be known of the sailing ship, and visited most corners of the globe. He was a typical sailor-man, both in his love of things which were shipshape and Bristol-fashion, and in his adaptability to strange conditions. Whenever he fell it was on his feet, and wherever he landed he made friends. There is a story that once he found himself penniless in Sydney, having spent all his money, with two weeks to put in before his ship sailed. He knew only two people – the Governor, who was a friend of his father, and a certain barman. The Governor was useless in such a case, so Jack became an assistant bar-tender, and spent a merry and profitable fortnight.

At the outbreak of the South African War he was in England, and, as he had to wait some time before the next stage in his training, he resolved to see a little fighting. He enlisted as a trooper in the Hertfordshire Yeomanry, and served with them till 1901, when he was given a commission in the Scottish Horse. Johannesburg in those days was like Piccadilly Circus; a man met everybody he had ever known if he waited long enough. For a little Jack was in the Criminal Investigation Department there; then he went on trek again, was wounded at Moedwill, was twice mentioned in despatches, and was promoted captain in 1902. At that time he had attained the mature age of twenty-two, and was probably the youngest captain in the British Army. The Tullibardines were very kind to him, but indeed no one who saw that rollicking figure could be otherwise than well-disposed. He spoke with an odd accent, which was not Cockney but the universal dialect of sailormen, and his talk was seasoned with strange idioms and subtle metaphors. I never heard a professional comedian half so funny as Jack could be when he chose. He was quick-tempered and as quick to forgive; eager for a row and any escapade of high spirits, and in every circumstance a purveyor of comedy. I remember one true tale of those Johannesburg days. At a dinner in the Club he said something disrespectful about the head of the Roman Church, and was promptly laid out with a champagne bottle by an irate Catholic Irishman. Next day he was visited in bed by his assailant, who came to apologize. "You must be a fool," said Jack. "If you love the Pope, why do you want to apologize? And if you don't love him why did you lay me out? "

JACK WORTLEY

At the end of the war he was given a commission in the regular army - in the Scottish Rifles. But he saw very clearly that home soldiering was not for him, so he applied at once to be seconded to the Northern Nigeria Regiment. In West Africa he was on the whole very happy, for his iron health made light of the climate, and he got all the shooting he wanted. He developed great skill as a transport officer, and early in 1903 was chosen to command the transport in the Anglo-French Boundary Commission - a responsible post for a young gentleman in his early twenties. It was an expedition after Jack's own heart, for the Commission made the first journey to Lake Chad since Barth in 1851. He had a remarkable power over natives (which he always attributed to the possession of bright blue eyes), and a genius for handling animals; and his sailor-like bonhomie endeared him to his French colleagues. He came home in the autumn of that year, and, still eager to extend his wanderings, got himself transferred to the 11th Sudanese Regiment and another quarter of Africa.

For the better part of nine years he served in the Nile valley, and did admirable work. My wife once happened to be with Lady Wimborne at Assuan when Jack was going up country, and was struck by the eagerness of every native he met to enter his service. He had the mingled firmness and humaneness which has made the British officer supreme in dealing with African races; and he needed all his powers, for in the wilds of the Upper Sudan he had much solitary responsibility. For long he was in charge of transport in the Bahr-el-Ghazal, and ultimately he became one of the Civil Commissioners. His duties took him everywhere from Khartum to the Lado Enclave and from Kordofan to the Abyssinian frontier. In 1910 he was engaged in a difficult punitive expedition, where insurgents had to be routed out of mountain caves, and received the Order of the Medjidieh for his work.

I saw much of him in those years when he was at home, and we corresponded with some regularity. I noticed that his old boyishness was departing, and that he was beginning to think hard about his future. As he once told his mother, with the shrewdness about himself which was one of his characteristics, he was far too apt to be absorbed in his immediate job and not to think of the next stage; but now the next stage was much in his thoughts. The truth is that he was homesick. He remembered England too clearly and he loved her too warmly to be happy at the prospect of an indefinite exile. When he was on leave he cast longing eyes on the English countryside, and his letters were full of a hankering after a greener land than the African bush. He was also too gregarious to be at ease in those vast solitudes. But he did his work with a cheerful stoicism and he found many alleviations in his life. One was the chance of sport, for he had all his father's passion for shooting and something of his skill. Once he shot a giraffe in a forbidden area and was asked for his reasons in writing. Jack gave as his excuse that the beast looked lonely! It was not accepted and he had to pay the fine. He used to read widely in those days, chiefly solid works of history, and now and then he found good company. One letter to me announced that his view of life was once more roseate, for he had got Alan Percy (the present Duke of Northumberland) and a case of vintage port.

In 1912 he came home, fell in love, had himself transferred to the Reserve of Officers, and was married in the autumn of that year. He was as proud as Lucifer, and was determined to make as great a success of his life in England as he had made of his work abroad. But it was no easy task for him to find the proper niche, for his experience and training were a little remote from home requirements. He tried various things without quite finding what he wanted, and his forehead was often corrugated and his eyes puzzled by the perplexities of civilization. He had the makings of a good business man, for he had strong commonsense and could toil like a beaver, and in time he must have found his feet. Yet for all his difficulties the two years before the war were happy, for he exulted in his new possessions, his wife, his children, and a household of his own; and it was pleasant to watch his gusto in entertaining his friends. He had still the sailor air and speech, and wherever he went a salt breeze seemed to attend him.

In the fateful August of 1914 he hurled himself—it is the only word—into the war. He hated the business, for he had outgrown his old love of vagabondage, and wanted nothing so much as a settled life. For soldiering in the ordinary sense he cared little, and he had never done any of the regular infantry training. But that his country should be at war and he should not be in the thick of it was unthinkable, and in the first days of August he presented himself at the War Office and demanded to be used at once. The next I heard of him he was A.D.C. to Sir Alfred Codrington at the camp at Luton Hoo. Then in November he blossomed out into a lieutenant-colonel in command of one of the Public Schools' battalions, the 21st Royal Fusiliers. Whoever was responsible for the appointment did wisely, for Jack was the ideal officer to train young men of that class. He created a most efficient battalion and in November 1915 took it to France.

It was some time before he was engaged in a major action. In the spring of 1916 he joined the South Staffordshires at home as second-in-command of their 2/5th Territorial battalion. He took it to France in November of that year, and presently was given command of the 2/6th battalion of the same regiment. Arras, in April 1917, was the first battle he fought in, and there he was slightly wounded. He was in action at Cambrai in the following November, where his battalion was all but destroyed at Bourlon Wood, six officers being left out of twenty, and 140 men out of 600. It was a fine performance, in which he showed great gallantry and resolution, and he was congratulated by his divisional general and mentioned in despatches.

The more he saw of the war the less he liked it.

JACK WORTLEY

He detested the mud and cold, for his years in the tropics had not prepared him for Picardy; he longed to be with his family again; he was too set in his ways and too independent to be happy under the ordinary military r é g i m e. A man who has been much alone and has all his life had large freedom of action takes ill with the ritual of modern war. But when I saw him for the last time in February 1918 I thought I had never known anyone so unchanged by campaigning. He was enthusiastic about his men, and the deadening life of the trenches seemed in no way to have dulled his eye for the human comedy. I think, too, that he was happier about his future. He had learned competence in his new trade, as he had learned it in his old African jobs, and was on the eve of being given a brigade. He liked the idea of ending the war as a General, and returning to the country life he had dreamed of with a good record of service. Certainly there would have been few more varied records than his to carry forward to the days of peace - war in many fields, travel in every continent, administration of new lands, and such opportunities of sport as have now become only a tradition.

It was not to be. The much-enduring Ulysses was not to come to port in Ithaca. On the morning of 21 March 1918 his battalion was holding the forward zone at Bullecourt, and in the misty dawn it took the shock of the German onslaught. We know how at that dark hour of our fortunes the thin outpost troops stood their ground from Arras to the Oise, and by their sacrifice enabled our armies to fight that great battle against odds which in the long run broke the enemy's power. Jack was of the race that defends forlorn hopes, and his men under his command did not yield. They were overwhelmed, and some time about nine o'clock their leader fell. At first there was hope that he was a prisoner, for there were no witnesses of his death; but when the few survivors of his battalion returned from German captivity it became clear that he had fallen in the first hours of the action.

Just as Cecil Rawling was the British private soldier in e x c e l s i s, so I like to think of Jack as the eternal type of British sailorman. Not the Royal Navy, but something far older than the Navy, the same breed as those indomitable Channel skippers who taught Drake his trade. There was always about him the large magnanimity of blue water. Like Ulysses he was a man of many devices, undefeatable by any trick of fate. He had the richness of heart, the whimsical fancy, and the perennial humour of the seaman, and something, too, of that seriousness which belongs to those who see the wonders of God on the deep. His end was what he would have sought. He had always a horror of being laid in a trim cemetery under a neat cross. On that grim March morning the guns of both sides made the place where he fell a tormented wilderness, and his body was never recovered. It was like a burial at sea. His grave was the whole earth, as the grave of a dead sailor is the infinite ocean.

Raymond Asquith

VI
RAYMOND ASQUITH

RAYMOND ASQUITH was born in 1878, the
eldest son of Mr. H. H. Asquith, afterwards
Prime Minister of Britain. He was educated at Winchester and at Balliol College. At Oxford he obtained all the chief University prizes,
such as the Ireland, Craven, and Derby Scholar-
ships, and First Class Honours in Classical Mod-
erations and "Greats." He became a fellow of All
Souls' College in 1902. He was called to the Bar
and had a considerable practice in Crown cases,
becoming ultimately Junior Counsel to the Inland
Revenue. At the time of his death he was pro-
spective Liberal candidate for Derby. On the
outbreak of war he joined the Queen's Westminsters and subsequently became a Lieutenant in
the Grenadier Guards, in whose ranks he fell in the
attack of 15 September 1916, during the Battle of the
Somme.

RAYMOND ASQUITH

THERE are some men whose brilliance in boyhood and early manhood dazzles their contemporaries and becomes a legend. It is not that they are precocious, for precocity rarely charms, but that for every sphere of life they have the proper complement of gifts, and finish each stage so that it remains behind them like a delicate and satisfying work of art. Sometimes the curtain drops suddenly, the daylight goes out of the picture, and the promise of youth dulls into a dreary middle-age of success, or, it may be, of failure and cynicism. But for the chosen few, like Raymond Asquith, there is no disillusionment. They march on into life with a boyish grace, and their high noon keeps all the freshness of the morning. Certainly to his cradle the good fairies brought every dower. They gave him great beauty of person; the gift of winning speech; a mind that mastered readily whatever it cared to master; poetry and the love of all beautiful things; a magic to draw friends to him; a heart as tender as it was brave. One gift only was withheld from him – length of years.

Great talents, to be pleasing, must be borne easily, carelessly. Their possessor must seem to be as other mortals, a little ashamed of excelling, careful to hide his light under the nearest bushel

lest it should annoy weak eyes. In that circle at
Oxford of which Raymond was the centre, there
was no suspicion of pose, unless it be a pose in
youth to have no pose. The "grand manner" in
the eighteenth-century sense was cultivated, which
meant a deliberate lowering of key in professions,
and a scrupulous avoidance of parade. A careless
good breeding and an agreeable worldliness were
its characteristics. It was a very English end to
strive for, and by no means a common one, for ur-
banity of mind is rarely the aim of youth. It implied, perhaps, an undue critical sense, and a
failure in certain generous foibles. Some of us
were men of the world too young; humour and
balance were prized too highly; a touch of Gothic
extravagance was needed to correct our over-
mellow Hellenism. Such a circle does not breed
Quixotes or reformers, and of none of us (except
myself, perhaps, who at the time was an ardent
Jacobite) could it be said, in the phrase of Villiers
de l'Isle-Adam, "il gardait au cœur les richesses
stériles d'un grand nombre de rois oubliès." I have
known men like Hugh Dawnay and Francis Grenfell who would ride on a lost cause over the edge
of the world. But our little Oxford group was not
of this kind; each of us would have rejoiced to ride
over the world's edge, but it would have been not
for a cause but for the fun of the riding.

Yet I would not have you think that we were
worldly-wise. We reserved our chief detestation
for Worldly Wisemen, for what we called "hey-
gates." To think of a "career" and to be prudent

in laying its foundations was in our eyes the un-
pardonable sin. It was well enough to be successful if success could be achieved unostentatiously
and carried lightly, but there must be no appearance of seeking it. Raymond, who won every possible prize and scholarship, must have worked
hard some time or other, but no one could say
when. He never appeared to work at Oxford, and
his letters during the vacations were full only of
sport and conviviality and unutilitarian studies.
An air of infinite leisure hung about him.

Again, while affectionate and rather gentle with
each other, we wore a swashbuckling manner to
the outer world. It was our business to be regard-
less of consequences, to be always looking for preposterous adventures and planning crazy feats,
and to be most ready for a brush with constituted
authority. "Booms" were a great fashion. Their
inventors were, I think, Hubert Howard and the
generation preceding ours, but we developed them
into a science. It was a "boom" to canoe an in-
credible distance between a winter's dawn and
dusk; to set out to walk to London at a moment's
notice; to get horses, choose a meeting-place,
mark down compass-courses and ride them out,
though the way lay through back gardens and
flooded rivers: to sleep out of doors in any weather;
to scramble at midnight over Oxford roofs; and to
devise all manner of fantastic practical jokes. To
stop to think of consequences was the mark of a
"heygate." All this, of course, was the ordinary
high spirits of young men delighting in health and

strength, which happily belong to the Oxford of every generation. The peculiar features of our circle were that this physical exuberance was found among men of remarkable intellectual power, and that it implied no corresponding abandon in their intellectual life. In the world of action we were ripe for any adventure; in the things of the mind we were critical, decorous, chary of enthusiasm-revenants from the Augustan age.

The figure of Raymond in those days stands very clear in my memory, for he had always the complete detachment from the atmosphere which we call distinction. He wore generally an old shooting coat of light grey tweed and grey flannel trousers; the laxest sumptuary law would have made havoc of his comfort. He had rather deep-set grey eyes, and his lips were always parted as if at the beginning of a smile. He had a fine straight figure, and bore himself with a kind of easy stateliness. His manner was curiously self-possessed and urbane, but there was always in it something of a pleasant aloofness, as of one who was happy in society but did not give to it more than a little part of himself.

He had come up from Winchester with a great reputation, and also, I think, a little tired. His scholarship was almost too ripe for his years, and he had already conquered so many worlds that he was little troubled with ordinary ambition. As the son of an eminent statesman he had seen much of distinguished people who to most of us were only awful names, so that he seemed all his time at

Oxford to have one foot in the greater world. Not that he gave this impression by anything that he said or did; it was rather by his whole-hearted delight in Oxford and his lack of reverence for the standards that ruled outside it. He had the air of having seen enough of the outer world to judge it with coolness and detachment.

Even in those early years his great powers of mind were patent to all. I have never met any man so richly endowed with diverse talents. In sheer intellectual strength he may have had his equals, and there were certain limits to his imaginative sympathies; but for manifold and multiform gifts I have not found his like. He was a fine classical scholar, at once learned and precise; he was widely read in English literature; he wrote good poetry, Greek, Latin, and English; he had the most delicate and luminous critical sense; he had an uncanny gift of exact phrase, whether in de-nunciation or in praise. His ordinary conversation was chiefly remarkable for its fantastic humour, but when he chose he was a master of manly good sense. As a letter-writer he was easily the best of us, but his epistles were dangerous things to leave lying about, for he had a most indiscreet and un-bridled pen. He could not write a sentence without making it characteristic and imparting into it some ribald whimsicality. We had a little club called the Horace Club, where the members read their own verses and supped in what they believed to be the Roman manner. The arbiter for each meet-ing was elected by lot, and usually contented himself with issuing a formal invitation. Not so Raymond. I transcribe his form of summons:

1. There being no authority discoverable in our Patron's Odes for the contribution of fruit and nuts sanctioned by former Arbiters, members are forbidden to bring either the one or the other.
2. It being known that our Patron produced his poems under the influence of endive and mallows

> ('me pascunt olivae,
> Me cichorea levesque malvae.
>
> C. I, xxxi, 15)

members may bring with them both these vegetables; or they may be provided by the Arbiter. But this is unlikely.
3. Should members wish to bring unguents, they are advised that the following have the sanction of our Patron; the ordinary or Assyrian nard (C. II, xi, 16) Malobathrum, a product of Syria (C. II, vii, 8) and Balanus (C. III, xxix, 4); the latter is also called Myrobalanus. It may be stated for the convenience of members that the cheapest variety is to be obtained in the country of the Troglodytes.
4. Wine will be provided by the Arbiter; who nevertheless ventures to hope that the self-respect of members, reinforced by the example of the Lapithae, to which our Patron has called attention (C. I, xviii, 7) will prevent their exceeding a reasonable limit in the consumption of it.
5. Members are earnestly requested to divest themselves of their Median Scimitars before entering the Arbiter's room; our Patron having recorded his opinion (C. I, xxvii, 6) that such weapons are inappropriate at social gatherings.
6. Members are invited to bring pet quails, if they feel that this would add to their comfort. Ladies may also be brought, but in the latter case permission must first be obtained from the Arbiter.
7. Members are further permitted to bring turtles or small horses: but it is hoped that this right will not be exercised.

As a speaker I never heard him in the political clubs, for I belonged to the Tory camp, and he, naturally, to the Liberal. But in the Union he was easily the most finished debater of our time. It was a hey-day of Union oratory, for Hilaire Belloc, F. E. Smith, and John Simon were our immediate predecessors and still took part in debates. Raymond and I usually spoke together on the same side, and chiefly on foreign policy. My efforts, I am sure, were solemn to excess, for in those days I was an ardent critic of Lord Salisbury: Raymond's were strings of brilliant and polished epigrams. He did not seem to seek to convince; smoothly, almost disdainfully, in his beautiful voice flowed his fastidious satire. There were no signs of careful preparation, and yet, had his speeches been printed verbatim, each sentence would have stood out as finely cut as in an essay of Stevenson's.

His politics were hereditary, not, I think, the result of any personal enthusiasm. He had a thoroughly conservative temperament, and loathed the worn counters of party warfare. Not greatly respecting many people he had a profound respect for his father, and much resembled him, both in his style of speaking and in the quality of his mind. He would not condescend to cheap-jack argument, and he distrusted emotion in public life. He was like his father, too, in many traits of character – his loyalty, his hatred of intrigue, his contempt for advertisement, and his unruffled courage. I do not think that at that time he had any strong political opinions (though many prejudices about political figures), except on the question of the Church. He detested clericalism, and like the Irishman at

Donnybrook when he found its head anywhere he smote it. I only once saw him in the Union roused to a real show of feeling. The matter in debate was whether some work attacking the Oxford Movement should be cast out of the library. The book was admittedly trash, but those who opposed its rejection did so on the ground that the reason alleged was not its literary badness but its opinions, and that such censorship over thought was intolerable. I can remember Raymond speaking with a white face and an unwonted passion in his voice. He asked where such censorship would stop. There were books on the shelves, he said, by Roman writers which poured venom upon the greatest man that ever lived. Were these books to be expelled? "I assure you," he told the angry ranks of Keble and St. John's, "that the fair fame of Caesar is as dear to me as that of any dead priest can be to you."

But he spoke best when he was merely fooling – after dinner, or at the meetings of a social club, or in the midst of a "boom," when the call came for oratory. During my "Greats" schools I had a free afternoon, and Raymond and I resolved to be American tourists. We bought wideawake hats, hired an open carriage, and with Baedekers in our hands and our feet on the cushions drove into the country. In some village the name of which I have forgotten we drew up at an inn, and Raymond addressed the assembled rustics on the virtues of total abstinence. It was the most perfect parody conceivable of a temperance speech, and it completely solemnized his hearers. Then he ordered beer all round.

I do not think he could ever have been called popular. He was immensely admired, but he did not lay himself out to acquire popularity, and in the ordinary man he inspired awe. rather than liking. His courtesy had no warmth in it; he was apt to be intolerant of mediocrity; and he had no desire for facile acquaintanceships. Also - let it be admitted - there were times when he was almost inhuman. He would destroy some piece of homely sentiment with a jest, and he had no respect for the sacred places of dull men. There was always a touch of scorn in him for obvious emotion, obvious creeds, and all the accumulated lumber of prosaic humanity. That was a defect of his great qualities. He kept himself for his friends and refused to bother about the world. But to such as were admitted to his friendship he would deny nothing. I have never known a friend more considerate, and tender, and painstaking, and unfalteringly loyal. It was the relation of all others in life for which he had been born with a peculiar genius.

I have said that he came up to Oxford with little ambition, and he went down with less. He stood aloof from worldly success, not from any transcendental philosophy, but simply because the rewards of common ambition seemed to him too trivial for a man's care. He loved the things of the mind - good books, good talk - for their own sake; he loved above all things youth and the company of his friends. To such a man it was hard to leave Oxford, for it meant a break with youth and the haunts of youth, and he had no zest for new and commoner worlds. In looking over old letters from him I find a constant lament that that chapter must close.

I fancy that no two friends were ever more unlike than he and I. He chaffed me unmercifully about my Calvinism, my love of rough moors in wild weather, my growing preference for what he called the Gothic over the Greek in life, my crude passion for romance. Above all, he abominated my Imperialism and my craze for far countries, for at that time he joined colonials and all foreigners in one condemnation. Empire-builders, Jews, callow enthusiasts, any one whose gospel omitted the art of life, were to him anathema. I had a notion that the world was a pilgrimage, in which you aimed at a goal and had daily to shift your camp. To him it was a little abiding city, from which you might make excursions, but to which you returned always of an evening to old wine, good books, and the same friends. "You scoff at the cult of Beauty," he once wrote to me, "in your coarse Scotch way. I grind my teeth when I hear people praise the machinery of Scotch education. Depend upon it, my poor dear soul-starved pedlar, the English public-school system is the only one which fits a man for life and ruins him for eternity. And commendation cannot go further than that, as you know well if you had the honesty to acknowledge it."

There was one consequence of this lack of ambition which the world may well regret. Except in his letters, he scarcely used his great gift for literature. A few poems are all that remain. One of these, an "Ode in Praise of Young Girls," written shortly before the war, is to my mind the finest satirical poem of our day, and I doubt if Pope or Dryden ever bettered it. He wrote many verses — he used to scatter them about his letters — but he rarely finished them. He and I once prepared a complete "Spectator," a parody of that admirable journal. The three middle articles, I remember, were on "God," "Bridge," and "Harvest Bugs." Raymond wrote the poem, a Tennysonian elegy, supposed to have been written by a well-known Oxford dignitary, "On a Viscount who died on the morrow of a Bump Supper." These were the opening stanzas:

Dear Viscount, in whose azure blood
The blueness of the bird of March
And vermeil of the tufted larch
Mingled in one magenta flood:

Dear Viscount, ah, to me how dear!
For even in your frolic mood,
I saw, or sometimes thought I could,
The pure, proud purpose of a Peer.

Upon that last sad night of all,
Erect among the rabble rout,
You beat your tangled music out,
Lofty, aloof, viscountial.

You struck a footbath with a can,
And with a can you struck a bath: —
There on the yellow gravel path,
As gentleman to gentleman,

73

RAYMOND ASQUITH

We met, we stood, we faced, we talked,
While those of baser birth withdrew.
I told you of an earl I knew:
You said you thought the wine was corked.

And so we parted; on my lips
A light farewell, but in my soul
The image of a perfect Whole,
A Viscount to the finger tips.

When I went to South Africa in 1901 Raymond had just taken his First in "Greats," and was reading law for an All Souls' Fellowship. We maintained a regular correspondence, and the sight of his bold, beautiful handwriting was the pleasantest part of mail days in Johannesburg. He wrote pages of delightful political gossip, and unveracious accounts of the doings of our friends, and ‑ very rarely ‑ news of himself. Here are two extracts:

"Eighteenth‑century methods worked well enough while we had a talented aristocracy, but we can't afford nowadays to limit our choice of Ministers to a few stuffy families, with ugly faces, bad manners, and a belief in the Nicene Creed. The day of the clever cad is at hand. I always felt it would come to this if we once let ourselves in for an Empire. If only Englishmen had known their Aeschylus a little better they wouldn't have bustled about the world appropriating things. A gentleman may make a large fortune, but only a cad can look after it. It would have been so much pleasanter to live in a small community who knew Greek and played games and washed themselves. . . . I hear you think I oughtn't to be up at Oxford

74

a fifth year. You are probably right, but, honestly, I haven't the ambition of a louse and I don't see why I should pretend to it. There are a few things and people at Oxford that I intend to keep close to as long as I decently can, and I don't care a damn about the rest. If one fell in love with a woman or believed in the Newcastle programme or had no dress clothes it might be different. But the world as I see it just now is a little barren of motives. . . . I suppose I may have what is called a spiritual awakening any day, and then I shall start to lie and make money with the best of them. . . . The law is a lean casuistical business and fills me with disgust."

.   .   .   .

"The bleak futility of our public men on both sides is a thing one never hoped to see outside the neo-Celtic School of poetry. The general effect is that of a flock of sheep playing blind man's buff in the distance on a foggy day. Rosebery continues to prance upon the moonbeam of efficiency and makes speeches at every street corner; but he might just as well call it the Absolute at once for all the meaning it has to him or anyone else. No one has the least idea what he wants to 'effect,' and beyond a mild bias in favour of good government and himself as Premier, nothing can be gleaned from his speeches. . . . He has started a thing called the Liberal League, which appears at present to consist of three persons – himself, my father, and Grey – backed by a squad of titled ladies, who believe that the snobbery of the lower classes is greater than their greed. I trust that may be so; they say there is a good spot in everyone if one knows where to find it. . . . As to law~I am in the position of a Danaid incessantly pouring into the leaky sieve of my mind the damnable details of Praetorian Edicts and the Custom of Gavelkind. If they didn't run out at once I think I should be mad by now. God knew what He was about when He provided me with a bad memory, and I am not the one to withhold praise where it is due."

.   .   .   .

In 1902 I tried to induce Raymond to come and visit us in South Africa. Lord Milner also did his best, but nothing would induce him to leave England. "What have you to offer me?" he wrote. "Certainly not those who are clad in soft raiment (we saw them at the Coronation!), nor do I imagine that any voice cries in your desert in a way which tends to edification." He was now a Fellow of All Souls, and enjoying himself, as appeared from the pictures of delights which he drew to lure me home, and his hilarity about politics. "No two people seem to disagree about anything~except Rosebery and C.B.; and neither of them has anything you could call an opinion, except about each other; in which opinion, of course, they are both right." Then suddenly he was heard of in Egypt, and we found ourselves in the same continent. He thought meanly of the Nile, the monuments, the scenery ("about as picturesque as a spittoon"), everything except the climate. "The sunsets are wonderful, passing from palest green through

76

every shade of yellow to deepest purple with a rapidity and precision which is more like Beerbohm Tree than the Almighty." He rejoiced to see a land where, he said, any kind of self-government was manifestly out of the question. At that time he was not enamoured of what he called "middle-Victorian shibboleths."

When I came back from South Africa at the end of 1903 I found that Raymond had cut loose from Oxford, and was already in London society the same distinguished and slightly detached figure which he had been at the University. He was reading for the Bar, and had plenty of leisure to enjoy life and see his friends. At that time I lived in the Temple with his friend, Harold Baker, and the three of us used to go for country walks of a Sunday and have periodical dinners at which we drank claret on the old scale. He had become even handsomer than before, and in London clothes he had a slightly ascetic look. Oxford was behind him, and he had set himself to make the best of his new life. He looked with a more kindly eye upon politics, for the Tariff Reform controversy had left him a strong Free Trader, and he began to speak a little for his party. But till he was settled in practice at the Bar he took neither law nor politics too seriously. He was not a whit more ambitious than at Oxford, and had still about him the suggestion of some urbane and debonair scholar-gipsy, who belonged to a different world from the rest of us. It was this air of aloofness which gave him his pe-

culiar attraction to those who met him for the first
time, and acquaintance did not stale that charm.
There was in him all the fascination of the unex-
pected and unpredictable. His wit flowed as easily
as a brook, but into curious eddies. He had a great
talent for acute but surprising descriptions of
people, especially those whom he did not love.
And his humour was oftenest the Aristophanic
σκῶμμα παρὰ προσδοκίαν. I remember one instance.
Someone, in one of the round games which were
then popular, propounded a stupid riddle: "What
is that which God never sees, kings rarely see,
and we see every day?" The answer is, "An
equal." Raymond's answer was, "A joke."

Then he fell in love and married – in July 1907,
the same month as my own wedding. He and I
gave our final bachelor dinner together at the
Savoy. Marriage did not, I think, wake his ambition as he once prophesied it might, but it regular-
ized his talents; canalized, as it were, a stream
which had hitherto flowed at random. He settled
down seriously to work at the Bar, with Parliament
somewhere in the future. He succeeded, of course,
up to a point. His father was now Prime Minister,
and he was naturally briefed in important cases as
a junior for or against the Crown. Of course, too,
he did his work well, for he was incapable of doing
anything badly. But I question if he would ever
have made one of the resounding successes of ad-
vocacy. For one thing he did not care enough
about it; for another, he scorned the worldly wisdom which makes smooth the steps in a career.

RAYMOND ASQUITH

He had no gift of deference towards eminent solicitors or of reverence towards heavy-witted judges. He would probably have passed, if he had lived, through the stage of Treasury junior to a seat on the Bench, where his perfect lucidity of mind and precision of phrase would have made him a most admirable judge – a second Bowen, perhaps, without Bowen's super-subtlety. But I do not think he would ever have won that commanding position at the English Bar which was due to his talents.

Politics were a different matter. Before the war he was adopted as Liberal candidate for Derby, and made a profound impression by his platform speeches. He had every advantage in the business – voice, language, manner, orderly thought, perfect nerve and coolness. The very fact that he sat loose to party creeds would have strengthened his hands at a time when creeds were in transition. For, though he might scoff at most dogmas, he had a great reverence for the problems behind them; and to these problems he brought a fresh mind and a sincere good will. His colleague at Derby, my friend Mr. J. H. Thomas, believed, I know, most heartily in his future, and he won golden opinions among the Labour men with whom he came into contact. It was natural, for he was the spending type in life, the true aristocrat who prefers to give rather than to take, and makes no fetish of a narrow prudence. Democracy and aristocracy can co-exist, for oligarchy is their common enemy. I am very certain, too, that in Parliament he would have won instant fame. His manner of speaking was as perfectly fitted for the House of Commons as that of his father. I can imagine in some hour of high controversy Raymond's pale grace kindling like a fire.

The War did not produce a new Raymond; it only brought the real man to light, as the removal of Byzantine ornament may reveal the grave handiwork of Pheidias. He disliked emotion, not because he felt lightly but because he felt deeply. He most sincerely loved his country, but he loved her too much to identify her with the pasteboard goddess of the music-halls and the hustings. War meant to him the shattering of every taste and interest, but he did not hesitate. It was no sudden sentimental fervour that swept him into the army, but the essential nature of one who had always been shy of rhetorical professions, but was very clear about the real thing. Austerely self-respecting, he had been used to hide his devotions under a mask of indifference, and would never reveal them except in deeds. That is the way of England at her best. Almost shamefacedly she moves to her sacrifices, but she will go through with them to the end. Raymond, being of the spending type, when he gave did not count the cost, and of the many who did likewise few had so much to give.

He began his training in the Queen's Westminsters, from which after a few months he was transferred to the Grenadier Guards. There he was perfectly happy. He was among young men again--the same kind of light-hearted and high-spirited companionship in which he had delighted at Oxford. In London I think the young Guardsman had held him in some awe, and to his friends it seemed not the least surprising result of the war that it should have made Raymond a second-lieutenant in the Grenadiers. He himself used to say that it was an odd trick of Providence to send a "middle-aged and middle-class" man into the Guards. Yet he had never found a circle where he was so much at home, and his popularity was immediate and complete. He was an excellent battalion officer, and so much in love with his new life that he sometimes spoke of going on with the Army as his profession. That, I think, he would not have done, for the Army in peace time would have bored him; but in the mingled bondage and freedom of active service he was in his proper element.

For a few months he was a member of the Intelligence Staff at General Headquarters. It was just before I joined that section, and when I went there the memory of him was fresh among his colleagues. But he did not like it. He missed the close comradeship of his battalion, and he had a sense that it was too cushioned a job for an active man in time of war. As he wrote to Mr. J. H. Thomas, he "sought no privilege not accorded to an ordinary soldier." So he went back to the Guards before the Somme battle began.

It is my grief that I never saw him during these months, and I was temporarily back in England on the day when he fell. In the great movement of

RAYMOND ASQUITH

15 September the Guards Division advanced from Ginchy on Lesbœufs. Their front of attack was too narrow, their objectives were too far distant, and from the start their flanks were enfiladed. It was not till the second advance on the 25th that Lesbœufs was won. But on the 15th that fatal fire from the corner of Ginchy village brought death to many in the gallant Division, and among them was Raymond Asquith. In his letters he had often lamented the loss of others, but his friends knew that he had neither fear nor care for himself.

Our roll of honour is long, but it holds no nobler figure. He will stand to those of us who are left as an incarnation of the spirit of the land he loved, in all its reticence and candour and richness and clean courage. "Eld shall not make a mock of that dear head." He loved his youth, and his youth has become eternal. Debonair and brilliant and brave, he is now part of that immortal England which knows not age or weariness or defeat.

HERE ENDS "THESE FOR REMEMBRANCE"
PRIVATELY PRINTED IN THE RICCARDI
PRESS FOUNT AT THE CHISWICK PRESS
BY THE MEDICI SOCIETY, LTD. AT
VII GRAFTON ST., LONDON
MDCCCCXIX

HERE ENDS THE FIRST GENERAL EDITION
OF *THESE FOR REMEMBRANCE*
PRINTED IN THE ORIGINAL TYPE STYLE AND
IN GARAMOND BY
RICHARD CLAY LTD.,
AND PUBLISHED BY
BUCHAN & ENRIGHT, PUBLISHERS, LTD
AT 53 FLEET ST., LONDON
MDCCCCLXXXVII